For Klara Sullivan-Campbell

Sincerely,

Jerry R. Gibson

Jan 4, 2013

# RECOLLECTIONS OF A MARINE ATTACK PILOT

## LARRY R. GIBSON

authorHOUSE®

*AuthorHouse*™
*1663 Liberty Drive*
*Bloomington, IN 47403*
*www.authorhouse.com*
*Phone: 1-800-839-8640*

*Published by AuthorHouse 7/6/2012*

*ISBN: 978-1-4685-7996-3 (sc)*
*ISBN: 978-1-4685-7997-0 (hc)*
*ISBN: 978-1-4685-7998-7 (e)*

*Library of Congress Control Number: 2012906497*

*This book is dedicated to my wonderful parents,*
*Jay Parnell and Jeanne Pauline Gibson.*

# FOREWORD

THIS IS NOT A NARRATIVE of my military career. Instead, it consists of fifty separate stories, as I call them, presented in the order in which they occurred. Each story stands alone as an anecdote or description of some event that I consider reasonably interesting or noteworthy.

These events occurred between thirty and fifty years ago. I had no written notes and have depended upon my memory for the contents and details of these stories. All of the events occurred as I have described them, or at least as I best remember them. At the same time, they are subject to occasional minor inaccuracies due to the passage of time, or due to my inability to describe them with the accuracy that they deserve.

Occasionally the description of some event, airborne or otherwise, might contain some unintentional, small error. My view is that such an error in detail, although undesirable, is not particularly important if the overall effect of the story is maintained. If some of my conclusions seem inaccurate to the reader, I emphasize that they reflect my own personal opinions or how I remember viewing the events at the time. These opinions and observations would not necessarily have been shared by others.

I have worked alone and have viewed it as something to do primarily for myself and my family. I emphasize that I do not consider any of my actions to have been heroic. Compared to what others endured, in whatever war you may consider, my combat experiences were miniscule; whether in intensity, danger, duration, or in description of deprivation. And I have nothing but admiration, respect, and appreciation for all who made greater efforts than those I have described.

A flippant saying I heard several times during my years in Vietnam went, "It's not much of a war, but it's the only war we have." Obviously, mankind would be better off if war were never forced upon any nation. But what would be worse than war would be for a nation to have its freedoms and life's blood taken from it without putting up a struggle.

Each generation is given its own challenges and responsibilities. I am glad that I can look back on my small role during the period of my service, knowing that I stepped forward with a willingness to serve. And I am thankful to have survived the experience.

Friends of mine who did not survive, giving their all, each flying his last flight much too soon, included Jim Buckelew, Al Hayes, Bill Arbogast, Norm Bundy, Bill Hawking, Jim Villeponteaux, Gene Kimmel, Phil Ducat, Dave Muschna, Bob Pixley, Jim Piehl, Bob Stone, Bill Wilson, and Jot Eve.

Larry Selmer and John Roederer, ground officer friends with whom I served, also did not survive. John Roederer and Phil Ducat, listed previously, were fellow officer candidates in my OCS platoon at Quantico in the fall of 1962.

Our nation owes each of them, and all others who have given their lives or suffered wounds for this country, a tremendous debt of gratitude. Our freedoms rest upon their shoulders.

Larry Gibson
March, 2012

# INDEX OF STORIES

# 1. THE MARINE CORPS LUCKS OUT

IT WAS SEPTEMBER OF 1960 and I knew I would receive my BS degree in Mechanical Engineering at the end of the coming school year at the University of Kentucky in Lexington. But something had been tugging at my mind for the last several months. For some reason I had always loved airplanes. Some young people want to become doctors; others want to become lawyers, etc. I had loved airplanes. Absolutely none of my friends had any interest in them, whatsoever. Where it had come from, I do not know. But I had loved them since I was a small child.

Although I had not been aware of it, I believe the desire to become a military pilot had been gradually coming to a head as I approached the end of my education. I could never have predicted when it would happen, or even that it would happen, but on that September day I made the firm decision to do something about my desire to be a military pilot. And just as there is a time for a baby to begin its move toward the outside world, such was the desire within my mind as it burst forth that afternoon.

I still remember having the specific thought as I left the university campus to drive back to the hospital where I worked for room and board. It was, "Well, I either have to do something about this desire to fly or forget it forever." I had always lived in Kentucky. If someone from there thought of military aviation, it would have been natural to think of the Air Force. No other branch of service would have even come to mind. So I was off to the Air Force recruiting office as I got into the 1952 Chevrolet my father had bought for my use a few years earlier.

I knew where the recruiting office was although I had never been there. It was on the north side of Main Street right about in the center of town. The university, however, was on the south side of town. For some reason

1

I ended up crossing Main Street and approaching the recruiting office along the street one block north of Main. When I arrived at the correct block, I parked the car, got out and walked to the nearest corner. Now all I had to do was walk one block south to Main, turn left and be there in less than a minute.

Little did I know as I parked my car on that street that afternoon that the location of that parking place was going to determine the path for the remainder of my life. It would determine what branch of service I would enter, where I would be trained, what types of airplanes I would fly, the number and types of combat missions I would fly, whom I would marry, what children I would father, and every other aspect of my life, including possibly how long I would live.

If I had parked on the south side of Main Street or if the parking place had been closer to the other end of the street, I would have been in the Air Force instead of the Marine Corps for those twenty years. Thankfully, God kept all of that hidden from me. I don't think I could have stepped from the car if I had known that so much was riding on what seemed to be such a mundane decision as where I chose to park.

The reason this was such a fateful decision is that as I walked toward Main Street, lo and behold, I walked right by the Marine Corps recruiting office! And they had pictures of young pilots standing beside jet planes in their windows. I did what probably any other red-blooded American boy would have done. I thought, "What the heck! Let's go in and see what they have to say about it." So I opened the door and walked inside.

I am sure I made that recruiter's day just by walking through the door. I suppose they had a quota to meet for the different types of positions they needed to fill. He would not have immediately known I was a potential pilot candidate. But I'm sure he observed that I was a reasonably well-built and seemingly intelligent young man, and that as I approached him, I looked him in the eye as I inquired about the Marine Corps flight training program.

I was probably manna from heaven to him as he found out I was a senior in engineering at the university and was interested in becoming a pilot. After answering some questions he asked me to take some examinations. So for the next hour and a half , I was engrossed in taking two multiple-choice exams. I don't remember much about their contents from those fifty-one years ago. But I'm sure they contained some mathematics and science and I would have done well considering my major in school. They contained a lot of questions about general topics in life as well. When I had completed the exams, he asked me to come back within a day or so for the results.

When I returned he was really pleased that I had done so well on the tests. He told me I had made a score of "eight-eight" which I interpreted as being perhaps 8.8 out of a possible ten. It was another forty years before I found out that those grades were in the Stanine grading system. In that system, a score of eight means the person being tested is in the upper eleven percent of those who have taken the exam.

My scores of eights were obviously far above the minimum acceptable score of five for each test. Still, the grades didn't mean much to me at the time beyond having passed the exams. The next step was to be flown to the Anacostia Naval Air Station at Washington, DC for a flight physical exam. What was really important was that I had commenced my journey to the skies. I knew I was finally on my way. I was going to fly jets for the U.S. Marine Corps!

The U. S. Air Force went to sleep that night having no idea they had just lost a future pilot. By the sheer luck of the location of the Marine recruiting office, and by the good break of an available parking space being closer to their end of the block, the Marine Corps had indeed lucked out in acquiring a future jet pilot. It was a good day for the Corps!

## 2. FAILING THE FLIGHT PHYSICAL

AFTER DOING WELL ON THE qualifying exams at the Marine Corps recruiting office in Lexington, I was flown to Washington, DC for a flight physical exam by qualified naval medical personnel. The plane left the civilian airport at Lexington, Kentucky for a non-stop flight to DC. I had studied planes nearly all of my life and of course knew the type of plane I was on. It was a Lockheed Super Constellation, a beautiful plane having three vertical stabilizers at the rear, an icon of long-distance passenger flight in its day. I couldn't have known at the time, but ten years later I would watch one crash into the tops of hangars at the Danang Air Base in Vietnam.

We didn't fly very high, perhaps seven or eight thousand feet at the most. I had only been in an airplane twice in my life and one of those times was when I was only eight years old. Our family had lived in Cumberland, Kentucky for the first ten years of my life. After the end of the Second World War, some enterprising young veterans had established an airport a few miles up the river toward Pine Mountain. It wasn't much of an airport, just a long cleared field paralleling the road with perhaps a rough building and wooden hangar.

There were perhaps five or six small airplanes there, with probably all of them being Piper Cubs, Aeronca Champs, and perhaps a Taylorcraft. Little did I know that some twenty-five years later, I would fly them all, and would own a 1946 Taylorcraft for nearly forty years.

My father had also been enchanted with airplanes and would take the family up to the airport occasionally to watch the planes fly. I remember the thrilling day when he gathered me and my nearly four year-old sister and helped place us into the back seat of an Aeronca. Within minutes we had lifted off and were climbing over the hills and valleys of the area. I remember looking down and seeing how small the cars looked.

I even remember who the pilot was. His name was Eddie Dobos. He was a young man, the older brother of Patricia Dobos, one of my classmates at St. Stephens Catholic School, where I attended until the family moved away in 1948. I must have been a reasonably aggressive young aviator, because I remember asking him to do a loop. He declined, saying it was because of my little sister Carol strapped in the seat beside me.

The story I was later told is that my mother suddenly realized we were no longer around and that she asked my Dad if he knew where we were. He pointed up at the little yellow plane in the sky and she was surprised to learn that two of her three children were having their first airplane ride. And soon we returned to the ground. I would not fly again until I was twenty-one years old, when I was taken for a short ride in a Cessna 172.

*Jay Parnell and Jeanne Pauline Gibson and their children; the author, brother J. Don, and sister Carol Jean in 1951*

And now, for the first time, I was on a big airplane that was actually going somewhere. It was a really great thrill to me and I looked out of the window at the ground all the way to DC, like a country boy on his first flight. A meal was served and I was so naive that when it was offered, I initially turned it down because I had next to no money for such perceived and unexpected expense. Fortunately, my seat-mate was more experienced than I and informed me that it was included in the purchase of the ticket. So I was able to enjoy the meal after all.

Some way I made my way to Naval Air Station Anacostia, right on the Potomac River, and spent the night, awaiting my physical exam the next day. The exam went well for a long time, as they prodded me, took a blood sample, and probably did other unkind things to my body. I even passed the eye examination, which was highly noteworthy.

And then I was checked for hernia---and I failed! I couldn't believe it. I thought I had a perfect body, regarding health issues. But the doctor assured me that I had failed the physical exam. When observing my degree of disconsolation, he tried to console me, saying, "Only about two percent of our nation's young men can qualify to become military pilots," and that I shouldn't feel so badly.

I later considered what he had said. Look at the requirements: college education, height between 5'6" and 6'4", appropriate weight, perfect vision, be able to pass a background check and on and on. As those who can't meet each of these individual requirements are removed from consideration, the number that is qualified for training becomes less and less. After all, the perfect vision requirement alone would probably kick out at least 75 percent of the population. Still, I felt badly.

My only consolation was that at least my shortcoming was correctable. I therefore planned to have the hernia corrected at the end of the school year and to attend Officer Candidate School in the fall of 1961. I related this to the recruiter when I returned to Lexington. He was pleased that I still planned to enter the Marine Corps for flight training, even though I had failed the physical on the first attempt.

He then suggested that I enroll in the Marine Corps reserves at that time. He tried to explain that it would be beneficial to me for pay purposes after I entered active duty. I was probably too suspicious and didn't want to obligate myself at that point and declined his offer.

That was a mistake! I was later to learn that the bulk of military pay is determined basically by two things: rank and what was called the pay entry base date. By declining to sign at this time, I lost a whole year of credit regarding this special date. It effectively postponed my qualification for a higher pay check by one year for the duration of my military career. Failure to take his suggestion probably cost me thousands of dollars over my career.

I received my BS degree on a June day in 1961 and entered the hospital for hernia surgery the next day. To do something with my time before entering the Marine Corps in the fall, I commenced graduate school. Then, after much consideration, I decided to complete my master's degree before entering the Corps. The recruiter was fine with it, particularly since I passed my physical exam when flown to Washington again.

And this time I signed the papers to join the Marine Corps Reserves in August of 1961. Establishing my pay entry base date of August 14, 1961 gave me one whole year of extra time for pay purposes during my military career. Now all I had to do was get through graduate school and be ready to join the Marine Corps in the fall of 1962. That is what happened, and getting my master's degree before entering the military was one of the best decisions I ever made.

# 3. MY FIRST MILITARY FLIGHT

AFTER CONVALESCING FROM MY HERNIA surgery during the summer of 1961, I was flown for a second time to Naval Air Station Anacostia in Washington, DC. And I found myself once again passing through the same halls and rooms I had traversed the previous fall. But this time I passed the flight physical.

I don't remember details from that day of over fifty years ago, but the exam must have been conducted on a Saturday. The reason I know is that Naval Reserve aircrews arrived at the field that evening for portions of their drill requirements. And these requirements involved flying, night-flying in this instance.

I had meandered over to the flight operations area, looked at the various planes and had entered one of the buildings. That is where I observed several reserve aircrew personnel as they prepared for their evening of training. They had separated into groups of four members each, and one officer, having only three members in his group, looked over at me and asked, "Would you like to go with us?" I was totally ignorant of what was going on and what was involved. But at the same time, I was innocently interested and eager to get to ride in a real Navy airplane. So I responded in the affirmative and was now part of a four-member aircrew!

Within minutes I followed my three fellow crewmembers out to a twin-engine plane designated as an S2F. I later learned that the plane was affectionately called a "Stoof," in typical Navy and Marine Corps fashion. It turned out that the official designation of many aircraft could be similarly altered to come up with some catchy and possibly descriptive title. Another fighter plane of the era, the F4D, was obviously called a "Ford" by its pilots, and so on.

After pre-flighting the aircraft, the pilot and copilot entered the plane first and took the front seats as dusk descended upon the airfield. I was directed to the left seat in the rear compartment and the fourth crewmember sat in the seat to my right. I put on the helmet that I had been loaned and figured out how to strap myself into the seat. Later, I responded when a communications check was made to all of the crewmembers by the lead pilot. Soon, I could hear the pilots going through their checklists as the engines were being started. After both engines were running, various checks of the plane continued, until finally the pilot called Ground Control for clearance to taxi.

As we arrived at the end of the runway, we sat there for a few minutes, awaiting clearance to takeoff. And that is when an interesting conversation commenced as the pilot spoke to me for the first time since asking if I wanted to go along on the flight. He asked, "What unit are you with?" I told him I wasn't with any unit, that I was just visiting the base for a flight physical. That must have been a shock to him, to realize that he had an utter, complete civilian in his plane as he was about to take off for a night training flight.

He quickly determined that I knew absolutely nothing about the plane, including how to bail out if required, or how to cope with any other emergencies that might arise. He told the man on my right to give me some instruction in these matters and we were soon airborne. In hindsight, the pilot should have taxied back to our point of origin and had me exit the plane. But he didn't choose to do so and soon we were taking off into the darkening sky over Washington, DC.

We must have flown for two hours. Most of the training involved using radar to locate a certain small ship in the Chesapeake Bay, and then making a simulated attack upon it. In the final phase of the attack, a brilliant light on the right wing was turned on, illuminating the vessel below.

I was reminded of reading about similar missions against German submarines in the Atlantic Ocean during the Second World War. The submarines ran by battery power when submerged during the day, but would surface at night to recharge their batteries with their generators. Our navy utilized small "Jeep" aircraft carriers to hunt down and destroy these submarines, similar to what our Stoof was training to do that night. I remember reading that the German sailors hated to see that light come on as they were being attacked. They called it "Das verdammte licht!"

Fortunately, our plane suffered no emergency. If I had been required to bail out, I would have been lucky to have gotten the parachute deployed while falling through the dark sky. And if I had come down in the water, I would have surely drowned, having had no survival training whatsoever.

But, like so many times in my life, I was lucky that nothing happened, and I was able to safely spend my first few hours in a military plane. There would be about 5,600 more of them, but that would be a little further down the line!

# 4. THE CUBAN MISSILE CRISIS

WE OFFICER CANDIDATES ARRIVED AT Quantico on the evening of Sunday, September 16, 1962, during the middle years of the Cold War. It had been nearly ten years since hostilities had existed between the U.S. and a communist country. That had occurred during the Korean War that lasted from June of 1950 until July of 1953. We all knew that Russia was our mortal enemy, but it never occurred to any of us that hostilities might erupt again at any time.

What happened was that Russia had secretly transported and installed nuclear-armed missiles onto the island of Cuba, just ninety miles from the shores of the U.S. Fortunately, they were detected by U. S. Navy reconnaissance planes. We were then successful in negotiation with Russia to have these missiles removed from the western hemisphere before they became fully operational.

I remember the time well. Quantico, Virginia was only about twenty-five miles southwest of Washington, DC. I remember the feeling of vulnerability, realizing that if a nuclear weapon struck the capital, we might suffer from some of the effects there in the Quantico area. There was also a feeling of impotence in being in the earliest phases of training and therefore of no value whatsoever if a shooting war had commenced.

Surprisingly enough, this crisis had an effect on our training. The reason is that the U.S. came close to invading Cuba during this period and this would have involved the Marine Corps. Because of this threat of war, some of our instructors were hurriedly transferred away from the Officer Candidate School to operational units that were preparing for the invasion. Our Platoon Sergeant, S/Sgt William "Spider" Rogers, was one of those who were reassigned.

That didn't bother us. Students generally don't like tough instructors. At that point we didn't particularly enjoy or appreciate Spider anyway, and were just as happy that he had left. Some replacement for him came in and the training continued. Our new platoon sergeant must have been some sort of nondescript type of person, because here, 49 years later, I have no memory of him, whatsoever. There didn't seem to be much of a personality in the man. And, although he may have enunciated his drill commands in a more standard manner, it just wasn't the same without Spider haranguing us from his Platoon Sergeant position.

After a week or two, the crisis tensions subsided, and the threat of nuclear war drifted into the past. And then one day, Spider was back! He certainly gave no indication that he was pleased about it. If anything, he was even more gruff and implacable than before.

But we knew he was back, and although we showed no visible sign, we were all just a little secretly (and guiltily) glad that he had returned. I say guiltily because I think we were a little ashamed to have been glad for such a tough man to have gone. It was as though we were a bunch of non-hackers.

When Spider again trained us with his odd "commands of execution" during drill, I think we all pulled our chins in a little tighter. And with a determination that did not previously exist, we were glad to have this no-quarter-given man back, leading us again!

There was no doubt about it. We were Spider's platoon and we were proud of it!

# 5. FAILING THE FLIGHT PHYSICAL AGAIN

I reported for Officer Candidate School at Quantico, Virginia in the fall of 1962. There were four platoons of officer candidates in the company and all fifty of the candidates in my platoon were hoping to become pilots in the Marine Corps. We had all passed a flight physical examination somewhere in the country before arriving at OCS. Having done so, I wasn't worried about that issue at all. In fact, I wasn't really worried about anything as the training was about to commence. In my naive state, I thought that officer training would be accomplished in some reasonably gentlemanly manner. I could not have been more mistaken. I was not going to be treated like a gentleman for a long time. It turned out to be far more difficult than I had anticipated.

We had arrived there in civilian attire around dusk on Sunday, September the 16th. After finding out which group we were supposed to be in, our sergeant formed us up into a semblance of a military formation. I still remember looking at this Marine in front of us, handsome in his immaculate uniform. He was around six feet tall, probably 175 pounds and square-jawed, the epitome of what a Marine drill sergeant should look like. At one point during his initial introduction, as he stood there confidently with his hands on his hips, he said, "Someday you may look as good as I do!" I sure hoped so!

I don't remember his name, mainly because he left within the first week or two. But we sure missed him when he was gone. We didn't like his replacement at all. S/Sgt Rogers was about the same height but more slender than his predecessor. He did not have the poster-Marine physique or the rugged good looks that our previous platoon sergeant possessed. The previous sergeant could inspire you with his appearance. S/Sgt Rogers could not.

To make it worse, the original platoon sergeant gave the drill cadence commands in truly great military fashion. S/Sgt Rogers, on the other hand, used different sounding drill command expressions that left a lot to be desired. His drill commands just did not inspire the platoon to great performance like the previous sergeant. A learning curve certainly existed as we tried to get used to our new platoon sergeant.

S/Sgt Rogers did not carry a pleasant expression on his face and he certainly didn't try to enhance it when dealing with the fifty candidates under his tutelage. He had a bit of a hawk-like visage to go along with a minor snarling expression and manner of speech. I don't know who said it first, but he quickly acquired the nickname of "Spider." We were stuck with the man. He was part of what we had to get through to become officers in the U. S. Marine Corps. We might not have liked it, but we were sure as hell going to give it our best shot!

About a month after our arrival, the platoon was marched over to the station medical facility for a new flight physical. None of us were concerned about it. We had all passed a flight physical before, so it should have been no big deal. Surprisingly, a significant fraction of the fifty candidates failed the physical for one reason or another, including myself!

I had been doing fine as I proceeded from one step of the physical to the next. Finally, I arrived at the location where our eyes were to be checked. I read all of the letters on the chart as directed and passed the color-blind and depth perception tests. The examiner then pushed what looked like a large metal Lone Ranger's mask up against the front of my face. It was the beginning of the end.

He asked, "Do you see that light in the center of your vision?" I said that I did. He said, "Tell me when it splits into two separate lights." He then began making minor adjustments to the mask. I finally said, "Now," and he removed the object from before my eyes. Examining the reading on the mask, he turned to me and said, "You just failed the exam." I couldn't believe it! One minute I was on my way to becoming a Marine jet pilot and the next minute I had been pronounced physically disqualified! I had no immediate recourse. I was told I could come back one week later for one final re-try.

It was a tough week to know that my dreams hinged upon the outcome of a single 30-second test of my eyes. I feared failing and devised a scheme to hopefully guarantee a successful outcome. I knew I had either called out too soon or too late. I had to guess which one and attempt to alter the result. Since there was no way I could tell when it was approaching the correct moment, I settled for waiting a little longer before giving the call. It was a 50% gamble, but it was my only hope since I wasn't willing to take a chance on what the reading might really be.

The morning finally arrived for the re-test. I had rested my eyes as much as possible. I sat down before the corpsman and he put the object to my face for the second time. Again he said, "Tell me when it splits into two lights." The single brilliant image remained as one distinct light for several seconds, and then it gradually began separating into two lights. I waited a few extra moments until it was distinctly separated by a safe margin and said, "Now."

He took the object from in front of my face, made the reading and set it aside. After entering the result into my medical record, he turned and said, "You passed."

# 6. OBSTACLE COURSE AT QUANTICO

Visiting the Meridian Naval Air Station this past summer, my wife Grace and I noticed the new obstacle course and I read about it a few days later in the Meridian newspaper, The Meridian Star. I was reminded of my encounter with the obstacle course at Quantico, Virginia when I attended Officer Candidate School in the fall of 1962.

Running the obstacle course was a regular part of our training and it was normally done in a competitive manner. The course wasn't the most difficult portion of our training, however. That honor was reserved for the dreaded Hill Trail. In full combat gear with packs and weapons, conquering the trail was a difficult undertaking even when in good physical condition.

In the last week of the program, Staff Sergeant Bill "Spider" Rogers marched us out to the obstacle course for the last time. S/Sgt Rogers didn't know we called him Spider, but that's what that dark-haired, slender, and tough man looked like to us. This was the day to determine the fastest member of the platoon. We were down to 35 candidates from the original fifty that had commenced nearly three months earlier.

We stood there in formation, our bodies at stiff attention when Spider said, "I want the ten fastest men to step forward." I was on the front rank and immediately stepped forward, suddenly realizing that I was the only one to have done so. "Back in the ranks, Candidate!" Spider boomed, and then he lambasted the platoon for their lack of confidence. It was the old, "You're all Marines! You should think you are the very best at anything and everything!" drill.

He then repeated the order, "I want the ten fastest men to step forward." Predictably, the entire platoon stepped forward this time. Spider was getting mad now, and bellowed, "Back in the ranks, Candidates! Let's get serious here. I want just the ten fastest men to step forward." For the third time, I stepped forward along with a few others.

We were ordered into the starting position and given the order to begin. I had put a lot on the line and gave it my all. Fortunately, I came in first place! I hadn't come in first on all previous occasions. There were two others who would occasionally beat me. But on this day, when lifetime memories were being formed, let the record show that I came in first place when it counted.

I've often thought that I peaked far too early during my 20-year career in the Marine Corps!

# 7. THE ALL-NIGHT WAR

WE WERE NEARING THE END of the OCS program at Quantico, Virginia in late November of 1962. Just another week or so and it would be over and we would be commissioned as second lieutenants in the U.S. Marine Corps! But we had yet another hurdle to get through. It was what was called the all-night war. There were probably a total of 150 candidates left of the 200 that had begun the program and we would all be out in the field together. It would be a tough night after a full day of regular training.

We took our combat gear and rifles and headed out into the hills via the Hill Trail that evening, arriving in the training area as dusk approached. Our platoon was divided into three groups, with one group remaining in a defensive position. The other two formed squads that were to roam through the dark night as though they were searching for the enemy. I was in the unit that stayed behind on defense.

A major was in charge of the overall company of candidates that consisted of four separate platoons. He happened to be in our immediate area as my best friend Billy Lindsay and I were being given our assignment. We were told to dig a foxhole in the middle of a Y-intersection in the dirt road and to man that position, facing back down the road. The major happened to be there and told us how to challenge anyone we heard approaching during the night. We were to call, "Halt! Who goes there?" If they identified themselves satisfactorily, we were to allow them to pass.

As the hour approached midnight on that cold night, Billy and I were in our foxhole, manning our post as we had been ordered. Billy had grown quiet and hadn't spoken for some time. Then I heard a faint noise down the road. Slowly, the sound was coming closer. Unable to see in the dark night, I guessed that it was close enough and called out, "Halt! Who goes there?" I heard the major respond, saying, "Major Johnson." As soon as he spoke his name, Billy's rifle went off with a loud "Bang!" He had been sleeping with his finger on the trigger and had accidentally fired his rifle upon awakening!

The major was livid! He came over and chewed me out royally. He said to me, "Candidate, you're not supposed to shoot me after I have identified myself!" After giving me hell for several minutes, he finally left our area and went looking for some other shortcoming to critique. All of the while, Billy had kept his mouth shut, naturally, allowing me to bear the brunt of the major's anger.

A few hours later, the other squads returned to assume the defensive position and now my group went out on patrol. As we moved along through the dark woods, I was at the tail end of the squad. Occasionally we would come to a halt and lie there resting for a few moments, our ears straining to hear anything that might be moving out in the darkness. I would lie there resting my eyes for a few minutes until it was time to move again. This went on for what seemed a long time.

And then I woke up! I awakened to find myself all alone in the middle of the woods with no idea where the rest of the squad had gone. I had drifted off to sleep while lying there and they had gone off without me. The man in front of me had not thought to make sure I was awake the next time they moved on through the darkness. I made a guess at the correct direction and walked for several minutes before coming to a dirt road. Turning left, I continued walking until I met two Marines coming the other way.

One of them was Spider, the platoon sergeant! He had been told to go and look for me and he was really mad! We turned and walked back down the road until we came to a large clearing where the entire company was formed up into its four separate platoons. The major didn't see us join our platoon as he was raking the company of candidates over the coals for all of their shortcomings.

After he had warmed up sufficiently in his verbal abuse, he finally hit the climax of his anger with the statement, "You have to be the most screwed-up class of candidates we've ever had. Of all the mistakes you've made, you even had one candidate 'halt me' and then shoot me after I identified myself, and now you've got another one lost somewhere out there in the woods!"

Little did the major know, that of the two candidates of whom he spoke, they were both one and the same candidate, namely me! Thank goodness he never found out!

# 8. A SERIOUS INTERRUPTION

I was commissioned as a Second Lieutenant at Quantico, Virginia on December 1, 1962 after three months of Marine Corps Officer Candidate School. I had been in pretty good shape when I arrived, but the physical demands of the training were tough even for me. Fifteen of the original fifty candidates in our platoon had been dropped along the way, most of them probably for inability to meet the physical training requirements.

Two members of our platoon were ex-enlisted and had previously gone through the enlisted men's boot camp at Parris Island which is notorious for its ruggedness. They both said that our training was even more difficult than what they had previously gone through. Presumably, it was because the Marine Corps could not chance ever having an officer falter when leading his troops. I had weaknesses in some portions of the program but I never fell out in any of the training and in fact won the platoon competition for the fastest time in running the obstacle course.

The toughest man in the platoon was Jim Galloway, a giant of a man to me at the time at 6'4" and 235 pounds. He had played football for Auburn University for four years. Jim went on to fly A-4's and I could never understand how he got his body into the small A-4 cockpit. Another tough guy was Ed Weihenmayer, who had played football at Princeton University. Ed received recognition among the newly commissioned officers for having the highest overall score of all officer candidates within the entire four platoons. Ed and I were in the same A-4 squadron in Vietnam a few years later. I couldn't hope to compete with men such as these if muscle mass were involved. But at 5'7" and 150 pounds I could sure as hell outrun and outclimb them.

And that is what I was trying to do on an afternoon of preflight training at Pensacola, Florida in early January of 1963. Nearly all of the 35 graduates of my platoon had been assigned to flight training. We weren't all in the same preflight class, however, and there were numerous ensigns in our class as well.

On the day in question, we were to do a shuttle run of 300 yards. It consisted of running sixty yards, stopping and running back, and repeating this until five 60-yard laps had been completed. We weren't all running at the same time, but in each group a spirit of competition existed. I was going to win!

When my group commenced the run, I was soon in front on the way to the other end. A quick reversal of direction and I was still in the lead coming back! My dominance lasted through several laps and then something odd began to happen. I was unable to maintain the pace. I became more and more lethargic as runners passed me by. I completed the run, running very slowly by the end, and had to go sit down, totally spent. It was the last event of the day and we went inside for our showers and dressed for return to the BOQ. I wasn't doing well, however. I had commenced throwing up and could only lie there waiting for enough strength to return to allow me to leave. I was really ill for some reason. I later woke up, if you can call it that, in the base hospital.

I say if you can call it that because I was in a semi-coma for about three days before returning to normal. I remember seeing my medical chart later and it referred to me as returning to an asymptomatic state at about that time. For you non-medics, that meant I no longer showed symptoms of whatever had befallen me.

Sadly, I had been removed from my preflight class. My new assignment was to live at the hospital while the doctors tried to figure out what had caused my problem. That didn't take long after I told them I had nearly died at the age of fourteen from Bright's Disease, also called nephritis. It was pretty obvious to them that my problem in the run had something to do with this previous disease. They did all kinds of tests as I remained there for several weeks. Finally, a decision board was convened. I was to be sent to the Naval Hospital at Bethesda, Maryland to be seen by a U. S.

Navy kidney specialist. A kidney biopsy was expected to be performed to assist in the diagnosis.

I spent six weeks (!) at the Bethesda Naval Hospital, undergoing many tests and simply waiting for the Navy to make up its mind about what to do with me. I was on an ambulatory ward with several other officers who were experiencing various maladies. So it wasn't that it was unpleasant. But by then I was having no difficulties whatsoever and wanted to return to the flight training program. The Navy's predicament was understandable, however. They didn't want to spend a million dollars training someone if a serious kidney disease could return at any time, or at least during some period of extreme stress. I finally shamed them into doing something by hanging a large sign on the foot of my bed that read, "I've been here for six weeks!" That spurred some action!

Hurray! They decided to return me to flight training! The doctor had never ordered a biopsy performed after all but instead wrote in my medical file, "---the problem seems to have been transient renal failure that has left no residual abnormalities---." I paraphrased somewhat but the underlined words were used and they were the gist of the diagnosis.

I was flown back to Pensacola on the regularly scheduled medical shuttle flight the next day. It flew from the northeast down the east coast and then westward over to Pensacola, making stops, picking up, and dropping off patients along the way. So, on a beautiful Saturday afternoon, March 30, 1963, I arrived back in Pensacola. I still remember having a few tears in my eyes as we approached the base which symbolized Naval Aviation. It was a pivotal moment in my life as I was being given another chance to pursue my dreams of military aviation.

Two days later on Monday morning, April 1st, I checked in at the Marine Aviation Training Support Group (MATSG) and was directed to report to the Preflight School. A new class had commenced that very morning and I was added to its roll. I was back in the world of the living!

# 9. THE PRE-SOLO CHECK FLIGHT

IT WAS A SIGNIFICANT FLIGHT in many respects. In the first place, you can never solo an airplane until you first pass the check flight. A broader view was that subsequent flight training in jets depended upon my flight grades. I could not afford to make low flight grades on this flight or any other one. This was obviously not a flight to be taken lightly.

I had been well-trained in my first eleven flights. First Lieutenant Tierney was a tall and fairly quiet instructor who had prepared me as well as anyone could do. I have learned over the years, however, that it doesn't matter how well an instructor does. It is ultimately up to the student to learn what is required of him, regardless of the subject.

I will never forget my first flight when we were leveled off at three or four thousand feet and he told me to take the control stick. He probably next told me to relax my grip! And I was flying! Well, maybe not by much. But at that moment the airplane had only one person telling it what to do as he had me make gentle turns left and right.

After a flight or two, I remember coming in on my first landing attempt. The ground was rushing by so fast! But as the days passed, landings became more commonplace, although perhaps always the greatest challenge in a day's flight.

Another demanding portion of the training was when the instructor would abruptly and unexpectedly pull the throttle back to idle, saying "You've just lost your engine. What are you going to do?" This could happen at two different times during a flight. It could happen at low altitude such as shortly after takeoff, or it could happen at high altitude when you would have more time to sort things out.

The responses were different for the low altitude and high altitude emergencies and I made up two separate gouges to help me recall what to do in either event. We students had so many different procedures to remember that we would make up something to help us remember the correct responses and perform them in the proper order. Each of us might devise a different gouge for the same situation. I simply took a word from each step in the procedures for each emergency and made a nonsensical sentence from the sum of those words.

Forty-eight years later, I can still quote either one on a moment's notice, probably even upon being awakened at 3:00 a.m.! "Glide grassy, prop. Boost gear flaps canopy!" spoken as though they were actual sentences. That was the sequence for the low-altitude engine loss emergency. For the high-altitude case, it was, "Glide up grass. Forward trim canopy boost trouble report!" again spoken as though they were actual sentences. I said these over and over until I could quote them in my sleep. It worked and I learned to respond quickly and accurately each time.

The day of the check flight finally arrived. I flew with a different instructor who didn't know me from Adam and who was prepared to give me whatever grade I deserved. The flight went fine as I performed the required maneuvers and responded well to the simulated loss of power by the engine when tested. It was time to show him that I could land the plane. There were about a half-dozen airfields available due to the large number of training flights taking place each day. He directed me to one and that is when the trouble began.

On previous flights my landings were generally good, certainly good enough to have no undue concern about landings on this flight. But for some reason I could not land the plane well at all on this day. He was patient enough as he kept giving me chance after chance to show that I could land safely. But finally, after my umpteenth poor landing approach, he said, "Get your landing gear up and let's get out of here."

My heart sank. I just knew I had failed the most critical portion of the check flight. But he didn't have me turn back toward Saufley Field, our home base. Instead, he directed me to climb to two thousand feet and turn out over the edge of the Gulf Coast, just east of Mobile. He allowed me to circle around and settle down for several minutes before directing me to return to the field for another try.

My landings this time were still not up to my usual level of performance, but he eventually said, "Give me one more that good and I will get out." After having done so, I taxied over to where another plane was parked. The instructor there was climbing out of the plane for his student, just as mine was about to do for me.

After climbing out of the rear cockpit, and with the engine still running, Lieutenant Miller stepped forward on the wing to speak to me through the open canopy. "Now don't go out there and bust your ass," he calmly said. I realized that he probably felt that he was taking a chance in allowing me to fly alone. But sometimes the fledgling is kicked from the nest even though the parent bird may have misgivings about it.

Like everyone that has ever soloed for the first time, it was a heady feeling for me as the plane accelerated down the runway. At the correct airspeed, I pulled back on the stick and the airplane was airborne! As I climbed straight ahead, I looked in the rear view mirror and saw the instructor's headset cord oscillating back and forth at the side of the cockpit where he had attached it. I was all alone! There was no one to help me get it back on the ground.

I made three landings as he had ordered and taxied back over to pick him up. He had rolled the dice and won. His student had not busted his ass. He would have had hell to pay if I had done so. I can hear him saying now, "Well, he was having some problems, but I assumed he could do it." And the Navy captain would have retorted like Captain Queeg in *The Caine Mutiny*, "You can't assume a damned thing in the United States Navy, Lieutenant! Because of you, this young Marine is dead!"

But it didn't happen. It may not have been my finest hour, but I got an up on the flight and ultimately my flight grades were good enough to get me assigned to further training in jets. And I went on to become a great Marine Corps attack pilot!

Well, at least I did my best. And my hat is off to Lieutenant Miller for having the patience and wisdom to know how to give his student every possible chance to get through his check flight.

# 10. "TAKE IT TO ANOTHER FIELD"

You would think that military flight instruction would take place in a quiet, calm, and near reverent manner as the instructor would quietly, patiently, and respectfully guide his neophyte aviator in the accomplishment of the desired aeronautical objectives. Sometimes it happens, and maybe even most of the time to some degree.

But it is often much more intense than that. Part of the reason is that working with flight students can sometimes be like working with children. I do believe that sometimes you could tell them to turn left and they would turn to the right instead. It can be frustrating at times for the instructor. I remember hearing Fletch Clark, a fellow Marine instructor, once say, "I don't mind flying with a student if he can fly. But I hate flying with him if he can't fly!" I quickly responded, "Gosh, Fletch, that's why they are here! They have to be taught!" His reaction was atypical, but it was still telling to some degree.

Flight instructor duty normally lasted for three years and instructor burnout was not uncommon. This could result in instructors sometimes becoming overly critical after seeing the same mistakes made over and over during their tour of duty. I remember observing a student make some sort of error once, somewhere around the year 1980. I said to him over the intercom, "How could you possibly make that mistake? I distinctly remember correcting Steve Maximov regarding that same mistake over ten years ago!" It was a joke and the student recognized it as such. But it illustrates the point about seeing the same mistakes over and over again.

Even my first flight instructor, Lieutenant Tierney, of whom I have spoken so highly, could sometimes resort to seeming intense anger in the air as he harangued me over some momentary shortcoming. I remember the first time it occurred. Up to that time he had always been patient and quiet in his corrections as he would make some suggestion to help me learn a given maneuver. But there came that time when all of a sudden, there was a burst of shouting at me for what he must have thought was my immeasurable stupidity or total lack of effort!

Instructors that resorted to this behavior were called, unimaginatively, screamers. On the ground they were perfectly normal human beings. It would seem unbelievable that they would ever resort to raising their voices at you. After all, you were a college graduate and a fellow officer striving to attain what they had already achieved. How could they possibly shout at you in the air as though you were an ignorant nincompoop, unworthy of any degree of respect at all?

But it happened. In the air, they became a terror! And there was not a thing you could do about it. Because after all, once back on the ground during the debrief, he was a normal human being again. It was like Dr. Jekyll and Mr. Hyde.

I recall a flight with an instructor shortly after my first solo flight in primary flight training. I had not flown with him before and all was going well for quite some time. Then, while I was going through the top of a loop, upside down, he pulled the power back to idle, giving me a simulated loss of power emergency. I rolled the aircraft upright to wings level, began going through my emergency procedures, and turned toward a nearby military field. All of this was done by the book and what was expected of me.

Then, I thought he said, "Take it to <u>another</u> military field." So I turned the plane to yet another military field within gliding distance. Then, with a voice and volume that indicated he was going berserk, he screamed at me, "I said take it to <u>other</u> than a military field!!" as though I were an idiot. I thought I had been doing what was expected of me and it made me angry that I was being shouted at so needlessly. I headed the plane toward a nearby farmer's field, as we called them, and set up for the simulated engine-out approach.

I left high key at the designated altitude above the intended point of landing. Dropping my gear and flaps, I passed through low key with 180 degrees of turn remaining before lining up on the final approach. I then passed through the 90-degree position and all was looking good. Continuing through the 45-degree position, I finally rolled the wings level as I continued toward the point of touchdown. I was lined up to land right down the furrows of the plowed field as per proper procedure. The farmer was on his tractor a few hundred feet off to the left of where the plane was headed.

The instructor pilot would normally say at this point, "I've got it," taking control of the plane as he initiated the waveoff to begin the climb back to altitude. But the instructor wasn't saying a thing so I continued the emergency landing approach. I was still so mad inside that I swore to myself that if he didn't take over the plane, I would land the damned thing in the farmer's field!

Finally, as we came lower to the ground than usual, he took control in the usual manner. But I'll bet he didn't know that I would have landed it right there if he had not done so. I suppose that was like cutting off your nose to spite your face, but that is how I felt about his screaming at me when I had simply misunderstood what he had said.

Well, maybe I wouldn't have.

Note---To hear a tape recording of the most famous screamer-pilot event of all time, go on the internet to "Youtube Saufley Field 1953." The event occurred in 1953 when four of the screamer's fellow instructors played a practical joke on him by taking his students' planes for the instructional flight without his knowledge. What follows is a hilarious recording (in two parts due to its length) that ends with the screamer finally telling the tower personnel , "Just go ahead and shoot them down."

# 11. THE ASSASSINATION OF JFK

I AM REMINDED OF AN event that happened just a few years after President John F. Kennedy was assassinated. In November of 1965, a massive electrical power failure occurred in the northeastern United States, including loss of power in New York City. When an event of this magnitude occurs, there are innumerable inconveniences for millions of people within the area of the power failure. Just think of how many people's lives were affected by the event on that day and evening.

The greater effect, however, was the long-range, unseen ramifications that it had upon many of those lives, in many cases effects of a life-changing nature. And, humorously, I read later of the spike in the number of babies born at about nine months after that time. It seems that with the electrical power being out, millions of people had little to do and went to bed earlier than usual. And I learned later still that this humorous observation turned out to be an urban myth.

The assassination of the president and the intense and near-constant television coverage over the next few days must have had a tremendous effect upon people's individual lives. Many of those effects have undoubtedly cascaded down through the decades to the present day, and will continue for centuries to come. Its effect upon my life is a perfect example.

I have always read that everyone that lived through certain significant events could tell anyone exactly where they were when they were first informed of these events. I speak of events such as the Japanese attack upon Pearl Harbor on December 7, 1941; the assassination of JFK in November of 1963; the day the Challenger spacecraft blew up in 1986; and the day of the attack upon the World Trade Center buildings in September of the year 2001.

I was turning four years of age in 1941, so I don't remember that one. However, I well remember the terrible Friday afternoon of November 22nd, 1963. I was a flight student at NAS Meridian on that dark and cloudy afternoon, and had just completed an instrument training flight. My instructor and I were told the horrible news upon landing. The next few days were filled with sadness for our nation as we mourned the loss of our young president. Whether one had democrat or republican political leanings didn't matter. The pain was felt by all.

The alleged assassin, Lee Harvey Oswald, was arrested almost immediately. However, in a bizarre sequence of events, he was killed while in police custody while being readied for transport from one facility to another. The series of events was totally unprecedented. Three days later on Monday, November 25th, the funeral procession was conducted on Pennsylvania Avenue in Washington, DC, culminating in the burial of President Kennedy in the Arlington Cemetery. I, along with tens of millions of others around the country, and the world for that matter, watched all of the events live on national television.

After the funeral had come to a close, I went for a long ride on a 650-cc Triumph motorcycle that I owned at the time. There had been no flying at the base that day in observance of the president's funeral. I drove off the base and out into the countryside, selecting the different roads at random while riding alone for the next couple of hours. I had no destination in mind and was riding for the pure joy and diversion that it provided. When dusk arrived I had ended up in the city of Meridian, twenty-two miles from the base. It was growing dark as I drove through the northern part of town, making my way toward Highway 39, the road leading back to the naval air station.

As I rode up the older version of the highway, I passed by a home I had visited one time previously, three months earlier. My best friend Norm Bundy had met the girl that lived there, although he had never dated her. However, in the short span of time that he knew her, I was introduced to her although nothing came of it at that time. And on a separate occasion, I was riding with him one Saturday forenoon when he decided to stop at her home for a short visit. The pretty girl named June wasn't at home that day, but we talked with her mother Julia McKee for a few minutes before continuing on to the base.

Riding by the home that dark evening in November, I recognized where I was and, upon sheer impulse, decided to stop for a visit of a few minutes. After pulling into the gravel driveway and parking the motorcycle, I picked the newspaper up from the yard while walking toward the front porch. I climbed the few steps onto the porch, walked to the front door and knocked. Mrs. McKee answered the door and I presented the newspaper, saying, "Paper boy." She started to go get the payment before I told her I was not the paper boy after all.

We had a good laugh and I reminded her of whom I was and that I had been there once before with my friend, Norm. I was invited in and saw the pretty girl I had met months earlier, and the rest is history. We went on to marry after I had completed flight training the following summer, and we had two beautiful children. Unfortunately, the marriage lasted only fourteen years and I will say no more about that.

The point is, however, that my life, and probably that of millions of others, was forever changed by the mindless murder of our president by Lee Harvey Oswald. I almost certainly would never again have seen the girl I eventually married if it had not been for the assassination of President Kennedy. This assassination caused a chain of events that was truly life-changing in my life. It may have had similar effects on perhaps millions of others.

Sometimes we plan our lives. And sometimes the events within which we live plan them for us. Or if they don't plan them for us, they at least put us into situations that change our actions and decisions such that our lives are forever changed.

If Oswald had not killed the president, or if it had happened a day earlier or a day later, the dice of my life would have rolled a different number and who knows whom I may have married or where I might be as I write this tonight.

# 12. HITTING THE BOAT

AFTER COMPLETING PRIMARY FLIGHT TRAINING at Saufley Field near Pensacola, Florida, we moved on to spend five months of basic jet training at Naval Auxiliary Air Station Meridian. The base later became NAS Meridian, a full-fledged Naval Air Station.

I still remember the day I drove into the Meridian area, arriving from Pensacola via U.S. Highway 45 from the south in July of 1963. Coming down a hill, I looked ahead and saw the skyline of the city in the distance. I still remember thinking to myself, "I wonder what this town will bring to me." Little did I know that it would dominate the majority of the remaining years of my life.

I continued on, finding my way to the base and checked in at the BOQ (Bachelor's Office Quarters), moving my few belongings into the room that I would occupy for the next five months. I remember seeing a few jets flying overhead, realizing happily that I would soon be flying one of them. I was a happy and lucky young man to be exactly where I wanted to be at that point in my life. A few days later, my class commenced ground school training . We were excited to know that we would soon be flying jets!

Airplanes, except for small civilian ones, are obviously complicated machines. The fact that they fly is merely the result of the interactions between their physical structure and the air through which they move. Besides some kind of engine to make them go, however, each plane contains an array of systems to make the whole thing work. These systems include hydraulics to power the flight controls and landing gear; an electrical system of generators and batteries to provide electrical power; electronics systems for navigation and communication; and a fuel system to store the fuel and supply it to the engine in response to the pilot's controls.

Each time a flight student advances to the next plane in the flight training program, he or she attends a ground school to learn about the systems in that plane. Only after completion of this school and passing the required examinations will the student begin to actually fly the airplane.

Our first experience in a jet plane was in the T-2A Buckeye. The "T" designation indicates that the plane was a trainer. It was nicknamed the Buckeye because the planes were manufactured by North American Aviation, located in Columbus, Ohio. The T-2A was a very well-designed trainer that had only one engine. The later models (T-2B and T-2C) had two engines but both were contained within the fuselage as all modern tactical jets do that have two engines.

If someone in the general public thinks of a multi-engined plane, they think of planes having one or more propeller engines or jet engines on each wing. If one of these engines were to fail during flight, an asymmetrical power (or thrust) situation would exist. This would be particularly dangerous just after the takeoff portion of a flight. When both engines are contained within the fuselage, however, no significant asymmetrical thrust exists in event of engine loss. The later models of the T-2 trainer therefore enjoyed the best of both worlds. These planes had nearly twice the amount of thrust, while at the same time possessing a huge safety factor, having two engines instead of only one.

The T-2 had straight wings, similar to popular civilian planes. This also provided a higher degree of safety, particularly in the landing phase of flying. Swept-wing planes are much more dangerous when landing. If the pilot gets too slow, the plane is more susceptible to stalling and loss of control than planes with straight wings. If this occurs when low to the ground there may be insufficient altitude below the plane to regain controlled flight.

I still remember my first day in aerodynamics class after beginning advanced training at Beeville, Texas in early 1964. We would soon begin flying the swept-winged F-9F-8 Cougar, a heavy, single-engine plane built by the Grumman Aircraft Corporation. As the instructor approached the classroom, our class leader called, "Standby." We stood up and the leader called "Class, attention!" as the instructor entered the room, saying, "Carry on," or "Seats," etc. As we sat down from the position of attention, he turned off the lights and walked to the back of the room without another word and switched on a movie projector.

On the screen in the darkened room, we watched a swept-wing jet plane (an F-4D Skyray) coming toward us through the 90-degree position in the landing pattern. It continued through the 45-degree position and by then even we could see that the plane appeared to be too slow with its nose positioned higher than normal. As the plane continued, it was approaching a stalled condition and the pilot was having difficulty with its control.

The F-4D finally made it to the runway, but in a full stall, impacting in a crash landing and soon was running off the left side of the runway. Within a few moments it was demolished as it impacted equipment near the runway and burst into flames. It was obvious that the plane was totally destroyed and the pilot killed. The instructor turned off the projector, walked to the front of the room and turned on the lights. Finally, he turned to face the class and said, "Welcome to swept-wing aviation." His point was well made.

Swept-wing planes were in our future in July of 1963, however. We had a lot to learn just in our straight-winged T-2A Buckeye. After transitioning into flying jets, we went through aerobatic, instrument, formation and night-flying stages of our training before returning to the Pensacola area some five months later. There, we joined squadron VT-4 for air-to-air gunnery training and carrier qualification aboard the USS Lexington.

Air-to-air gunnery was a blast! After the flight of four T-2A's arrived in the training area out over the gulf, a gunnery pattern was established with the planes attacking the target one at a time as they flew through the pattern. A tractor plane (another T-2A) pulled a target called the banner by a long cable. It was sort of like screen-door wire that would show the marks made by the bullets that passed through it. The planes carried bullets with their noses painted in different colors so we could later see if we had hit the target, and if so, how many times.

On our first flight, our gunnery instructor would fly the plane from the front seat. We watched from the rear seat as he demonstrated how the pattern was to be flown. The planes were armed with a single fifty-caliber machine gun on each wing. The instructor would fire at the target on this first flight whereas the student would later have about four flights in which they would get to fire. There was a standing bet between the instructors and their students about the number of hits they would achieve. The instructor would bet that he would get more hits during his one firing flight than the student would get in all four of his firing flights combined. For the instructor's flight, it was a "wheels in the well" bet. If his plane got airborne and for some reason he did not get to fire, that was just tough! It could happen for a variety of reasons. Even if his guns failed to work, that was still just tough!

My instructor, Lt. Fitzgerald, got about a dozen hits on his firing flight. I later accumulated about eight hits, as I recall, so he won his bet. But at least I was gaining on him. And I think I had one flight when the guns didn't work, at that.

We would usually have four planes in the gunnery pattern out over the Gulf, taking turns making firing passes at the banner. A lot of coordination was required by the pilots to keep the gunnery pattern functioning properly. It probably also took a lot of guts for the tractor pilot to fly along straight and level, pulling the target, while solo students were firing fifty-caliber machine guns in his general direction. I remember one occasion when the tractor plane returned with a bullet hole through its vertical stabilizer! I probably wasn't the guilty party, but who knows?

Then came carrier-qualification training, something entirely new. Of course, we had landed hundreds of times, using the same procedures and all, but going to the actual carrier was still a very big thing. For maybe about ten flights, we flew out to an airfield in a nearby USAF training area. We would arrive and practice landings with an LSO (Landing Signal Officer) standing by the end of the runway. He would observe our performance, critique, and grade each landing we made. A more extensive analysis of our landing performance would be conducted when we were back on the ground. After refueling, we would repeat the training cycle until getting down to just enough fuel to get back to NAS Pensacola.

The outlying field was way out in the boonies on the nearby Eglin Air Force Reservation. When we students were told to depart the field, we would raise the landing gear and flaps after our last landing and accelerate straight ahead, holding it low over the trees. We were alone in the plane and could get away with a little free flat-hatting as it was called. We would then pull up into a soaring high-angle climb, feeling like we were real jet pilots!

Finally the day came to "hit the boat," as the expression went. We were well-briefed on all of the procedures, but I still remember the apprehension as I climbed into the plane all alone that morning. I can't say it was fear, but there was certainly a realization that this was a significant event. Our flight of four T-2A Buckeyes took off and before long we were circling over the USS Lexington, a carrier that had seen combat action against the Japanese during the Second World War. We were perhaps some thirty or forty miles out in the Gulf and soon it was our turn to come down for our landings.

We entered the break over the carrier and turned downwind, dropping our gear and flaps, but keeping our arresting hook in the up position. I still remember the first touch and go landing on the carrier. The impact was surprisingly soft. Always before, we had landed on the unyielding concrete. But here, the carrier was moving and the relative velocity between the ship and plane was less than we had experienced before, resulting in a comparatively soft landing impact on the carrier deck. After a few successful approaches, the LSO told us to drop our tail-hooks for our arrested landings. We had been trained to go to full power upon touchdown. If we had missed a cable the plane would thus already be at full power to lift off for another try. If we had caught an arresting wire, the plane would still have been stopped.

After landing, we taxied forward under the direction of a deck-hand and into position to be catapulted back into the air. Once into position, the Catapult Officer would give us the windup signal and we would add full power to the aircraft. After checking our engine instruments, we would look at him, salute, and then look back straight ahead, awaiting the catapult. It was an unbelievable experience! It literally took your breath for approximately two seconds as you were accelerated to about 110 knots and found yourself flying off the end of the carrier.

We completed our four arrested landings and catapulted takeoffs and flew back to NAS Pensacola. I will never forget the feeling as I made the final landing approach back at home field. Coming through the "90," I still remember thinking to myself, "This is so easy!"

After all, "I had just hit the boat!"

# 13. THE GRUMMAN IRON WORKS

The Grumman Aircraft Corporation has had a long history of building aircraft for the U. S. Navy. During the mid-1930's, they had built the first airplane for the Navy that could retract its wheels, thereby reducing the aerodynamic drag on the aircraft. Predictably, it was also the first Navy plane that some unfortunate Navy pilot landed with his landing gear in the up position. In fairness, it has been said there are two kinds of pilots, those who have landed "gear up" and those that eventually will if they fly long enough. I didn't fly that long.

When the Second World War commenced in December of 1941, the Grumman F-4F Wildcat was the top fighter plane in the U.S. Navy inventory. In true Grumman tradition, it was built like an airborne tank. I read once that during its development at the Long Island factory, an arresting hook had broken under the stress of an arrested landing. The president of the company emphatically demanded that his engineers redesign the hook so it would never happen again. They did so, to the extent that on at least one occasion, the entire tail of the plane broke off while the hook absorbed the stress, none the worse for the wear.

Everyone knows about the Smithsonian Institution Museum in Washington, DC. Relatively few, however, know about the Silverhill facilities nearby in Maryland. The Smithsonian owns so much historic material that it cannot all be displayed. The excess material is therefore stored in large buildings at the Silverhill facility. I was fortunate enough to get to tour those facilities in 1973. There were aircraft there from all of the wars, including a beautiful Fokker D-7, the number one German fighter aircraft of World War One.

But what impressed me the most were two World War II fighters sitting there side by side in that enormous hangar. They were an F-4F Wildcat and a Japanese Zero. These two planes had fought one another in violent air battles during the early years of the war, as each side struggled to achieve air superiority. The Japanese found early on that the Wildcat was difficult to bring down, even after it had absorbed many rounds of machine gun fire. The Zero, on the other hand, would come apart or burst into flames relatively easily with many fewer rounds.

I walked up to those two airplanes and pounded the heel of my fist against the side of the Wildcat. It was like hitting a stone wall. Doing the same to the Zero, it was similar to hitting the side of a Cessna 150, the cheapest Cessna civilian airplane made during the 1960's and 70's. I may be exaggerating somewhat but the point is valid.

They were designed with different philosophies in mind. Recall the president of the Grumman Corporation. He wanted an aircraft that was strong in every aspect of design because he knew the planes would undergo harsh and stressful treatment during combat. He wanted his pilots to be protected by the strength of the planes that they flew.

The Japanese engineers, on the other hand, set out to build a fighter plane having the biggest bang for the buck and with the minimum amount of material. By doing so, an engine of less power could also be used. This afforded greater range and endurance than a more powerful engine would have allowed, while still providing high speed and a good rate-of-climb capability.

Life everywhere is a compromise and never more so than in the design of a fighter plane. A plane could probably be built that no weapon would ever bring down, but it might never make it off the ground due to its excessive weight.

The Republic Aviation Company was also well known for making its aircraft extremely heavy. During WW II its best fighter plane was the P-47 Thunderbolt, weighing in at 14,000 pounds, roughly twice the weight of the F-4F Wildcat. A standard joke was, "If someone built a runway reaching completely around the world, Republic Aviation would build an aircraft that would require every bit of it to become airborne!"

When I arrived at NAAS Beeville, Texas for advanced flight training in early 1964, the F-9F-8 Cougar was the first plane I flew. It was an even heavier-built plane than the F-4F which had long preceded it. Of course, this was due to its much higher speed capability and the higher aerodynamic loads that these speeds imposed. It was a swept-wing version of the F-9F-2 Panther jet that the Navy had flown from carriers during the Korean War.

An acquaintance of mine was flying an F-9 one night during that spring. After a touch and go landing on that dark night, he was climbing straight ahead when the tower radioed to him, "Your traffic is breaking overhead." The term "traffic" referred to the planes that he was to follow as he turned downwind for his next landing. "Breaking overhead" meant they were entering the landing pattern at an altitude above him and he would have to look up to see where they were.

Unfortunately, he was still close to the ground and as he looked up, he inadvertently pushed slightly forward on the control stick, causing the plane to nose over into a shallow descent. As he continued to watch for his traffic, the plane touched down onto the sandy terrain off the end of the runway. He came to a "smooth, controlled stop" as the plane decelerated from some 150 mph to zero, sliding through the yielding sand. During the course of the adventure, he shut the engine down and upon stopping, opened the canopy and stepped from the airplane!

He was lucky. There probably was not another jet plane in the world that would have held together in such a crash landing, enabling the pilot to nonchalantly step from it at the end of such an extraordinary ride.

Once again, the notorious Grumman Iron Works had saved a young Naval Aviator!

# 14. MY LAST BAD LANDING

It was around April of 1964 and I was about half-way through advanced jet flight training at NAAS Beeville, Texas. I was flying that day with a Navy Lieutenant Commander with whom I had flown before. I had not done well on that flight and I was destined to repeat the poor performance today, although l didn't know it until the very end of the flight.

I don't remember what we did on the training mission, but we eventually returned to the field for landing practice before making our final landing. I entered the landing pattern by coming into the break at 300 knots, turning downwind while dropping my landing gear and extending the flaps. During the downwind leg, I went through the landing checklist and gave my radio call to the tower at the 180-degree position. Up to then I was doing fine.

Coming through the 90 and the 45, everything continued looking good. A few moments later I visually picked up what we called the "ball," indicating that I was on glide slope. I rolled wings level in the groove, as it was called, and felt that I was nicely set up to make a good landing, hoping thereby to redeem myself in the eyes of my instructor pilot in the back seat.

I was lined up well coming down the glide slope and making good corrections for the minor right cross-wind. Meanwhile, I was doing a great job of keeping the ball centered on the mirror at the side of the runway. This indicated that I was remaining on glide slope. The air was smooth on this beautiful day and I was bringing the large, heavy F-9 Cougar in towards a nice landing.

I continued toward the intended point of touchdown, still maintaining lineup right down the center of the runway and just doing a really great job of staying on the glide slope. Man, I was looking so good that I probably thought I should be giving lessons myself!

And then, as I neared the end of the runway, still maybe a hundred feet above the ground, I heard my instructor pilot say, "I've got it!" as he added full power. Like all flight students everywhere, I immediately released all of the controls as we were trained to do. The instructor was now flying the plane.

I noticed that despite his having added full power, the plane continued to descend for several seconds before the aerodynamic lift and engine thrust combined to cause the plane to level out and finally begin climbing. What had I done wrong, I wondered?

The instructor then said, "You were completely ignoring your 'angle of attack' gauge. We were approaching a stall and I kept hoping you would catch it yourself but you didn't. I finally had to take control to keep us from stalling and crashing at the end of the runway."

I understood immediately. I knew that to land a plane, there were three things that had to be maintained: lineup, glide slope, and angle of attack. I was concentrating so hard upon doing well that, although I was doing a very good job on the first two, I had completely forgotten the third one. The angle of attack gauge was the gauge that the pilot had to monitor to keep the plane from slowing to a stall and I had completely ignored it.

I was totally embarrassed. If he had not taken control of the plane, I could possibly have stalled and crashed the plane. Maybe I would have caught it in another moment, but it was getting close to the point of no return. The laws of physics are neither to be taken lightly nor to be ignored. There finally comes a time when it is too late and even application of full power is not enough to prevent a crash.

I don't remember the debrief after the flight. Like I said, I had failed to impress him before and I sure failed to impress him that day. He probably wondered how I was managing to stay alive as well as I was. It certainly taught me a good lesson, however, one that I should not have had to be learning by that point in my training. I'm just glad that I had an instructor in the back seat that day.

But hey! We all make mistakes. And I will tell you one more thing. That was the last bad landing I ever made and I would be flying for the next nineteen years!

# 15. LOSING A FRIEND

THE LAST AIRCRAFT THAT WE flight students flew before receiving our wings was the F-llF Tigercat. It was a beautiful and sleek swept-wing plane and had been used by the Blue Angels demonstration team for several years at that time. It was one of a long line of "Cats" built by the Grumman Aircraft Corporation (Grumman Iron Works) for the U.S. Navy. It wasn't the last one, however, as The F-14 Tomcat would come along some ten years later and serve the Navy for over thirty years.

But getting to fly the F-11F presented some real novelties from the student viewpoint. In the first place, it was the first plane we would fly as students that contained only one seat! Our first flight in this plane would be a solo flight. Heretofore, we had always had an experienced instructor in the back seat during our first flight. Having him back there provided a large safety factor. A little perspective might be helpful. Compared to our flying ability as students, the instructors were all "Chuck Yeager's." The aura surrounding the flight instructor was even called the "God in the rear cockpit" syndrome. The point was that he could do no wrong. He could save you from anything!

In practice, it didn't always work that way. I recall the surprise and puzzling shock during primary training in the little prop-driven T-34 when an instructor and student were both killed during a training flight. I don't recall what happened, but it served to remind us that we were in a serious business if it could happen even with an instructor on board.

The other difference was that the F-11F had an afterburner! An afterburner is basically a mechanism that shoots raw jet fuel into the exhaust pipe and adds a significant amount of thrust to the plane. On the other hand, the plane is burning fuel at a prodigious rate when the afterburner is being used! Still, to us students, it was quite a thrill to be taking off solo on our first flight in the plane, and being kicked in the butt by an afterburner at the same time!

Although we were alone in the plane for the first flight, a flight instructor was assigned as a chase pilot to accompany us. He was there to observe us through our different maneuvers at altitude and to provide some margin of safety when we returned to land.

One final interesting aspect of the flight was that this would be the first time we flew supersonic, that is, faster than the speed of sound. That was done by climbing up to about 35,000 feet, nosing over into a slight dive and igniting the afterburner. After achieving perhaps Mach 1.2 or so, the power would be reduced and we would go on to other maneuvers.

Finally, we would return to the field, being allowed to make only one landing on our first flight. The chase pilot would be flying alongside the student as he entered the break over the field and would drop his gear and flaps along with the student. He would then maintain a loose formation position as the student came downwind to set up for the landing. Coming off the 180-degree position, the instructor would be just to the outside of the turn, monitoring the progress of the approach. If he thought it necessary, he could direct the student to execute a waveoff and set up for another landing attempt.

One July afternoon in 1964 I was returning from one of my last flights as a flight student. I was only a few days away from being designated a Naval Aviator and still remember my landing that day on runway "13" (spoken "one Three") at NAS Beeville, Texas. As I came through the "45" (45 more degrees to go to line up with the runway), I passed over a large patch of trees. It was a hot summer day in Texas and the air was cooler under the trees, causing a downdraft in that area.

I wasn't looking at the trees at that moment but I felt the plane commence a sink rate as I flew over them and compensated by adding power to the aircraft. I passed on through the downdraft, readjusted the power, and landed the plane without incident.

Minutes later I had climbed down out of the plane and was walking back toward the hangar when I saw a large column of black smoke. It was rising from the area of the 45 on the approach end of the runway where I had just landed. Within a few minutes, we learned that one of the students in our squadron had just crashed his F-11F and had been killed.

The student was Jim Buckelew, a Marine lieutenant friend of mine. He was about two weeks behind me in the training program and was flying his first flight in the F-11F! Whereas I had accumulated sufficient experience and familiarity with the plane to recognize the sink rate and add power promptly, he was slower to sense the sink rate and paid the ultimate price.

Upon finally feeling the airplane sinking toward the ground, he added power but it was too late. He probably went to full power and afterburner as well. But once a plane is in a stall, all of the power available would have been inadequate to restore the plane to safe flight. As it stalled, it rolled off to the left and Jim attempted to eject. But the plane was no longer upright and he was killed in the ejection attempt.

There was nothing the chase instructor could do as he was probably flying one hundred feet away to Jim's right. His plane may have been far enough away to avoid the sink rate while passing over the trees. If so, he could not have known to warn Jim.

The issue came down to the fact that, while flying an unfamiliar aircraft for the first time, he was faced with a downdraft situation at the worst possible moment. There was not enough altitude under the plane to enable him to recover normal flight. It was a case of ,"There but for the grace of God go I."

I can only give thanks that better flight conditions had existed two weeks earlier when I had flown my first flight in the beautiful F-llF aircraft.

## 16. THEY CALL ME "SLICK"

It was September of 1964 and I had been in an A-4 Skyhawk squadron for only a month. The squadron had been steadily adding other newly-graduated pilots like me. Most of us had gone straight from Officer Candidate School at Quantico, Virginia into the U. S. Navy flight training program and this was our first assignment in the real Marine Corps. As newly-designated Naval Aviators, we were on top of the world as brand-new Marine Corps jet pilots.

Several of us lieutenants were standing in the ready room one afternoon when a new pilot arrived. He was a good-looking Marine, but then again, all Marines are good-looking. This young Marine officer, however, truly was a good-looking young man. Six feet tall and maybe an inch, perhaps 185 pounds of well-built young manhood and a cocky step like all of the rest of us. He was the epitome of what a young Marine Corps officer should look like. As he introduced himself, he gave his name and added, "They call me 'Slick.'"

So, there! Not only did we have a brand new squadron pilot, but he had arrived with his own self-appointed, image-enhancing nickname. Slick he was, from then on.

Slick really had it all. Rugged good looks, a fairly good personality, a seeming aggressiveness required of all Marine Corps jet pilots, and a beautiful wife who was well-accepted and liked by all of the young officer's wives. And, like most of us young pilots, he was brimming over with high self-esteem.

Being the good-looking, well-built, and fairly rugged-looking guy that he was, he had probably always done well and probably looked up to in everything he had ever attempted. Like the rest of us, he had received his college degree and earned his commission as an officer in the U.S. Marine Corps. And he had now additionally received his wings as a Naval Aviator, thereby joining one of the most elite groups of pilots in the military world. I would imagine he expected to continue doing as well as a Marine Corps pilot as he had done in everything else.

But he didn't stand out. And there was nothing wrong with that. Once we became acquainted with our new airplane, the A-4 Skyhawk, we all had pretty much the same amount of success with it. The more experienced pilots had an advantage at first. But the new lieutenants that joined with me, or nearly at the same time, gradually got better until we could bomb and shoot as well as they could, on the average.

Like everyone else, Slick would have loved to have stood out in the bombing and shooting that we did in our day-to-day training in our Skyhawks. But he was just another young attack pilot that was slowly improving his skills, like the rest of us. On the plus side, he was competent and gave every indication that when the chips were down, he would have put his ordnance on the target just like everyone else, or gone down trying.

After about a year in the squadron, I remember hearing him saying in conversation that he really should have been a fighter pilot, because that is where his flying skills truly lay! I thought at the time that the statement was intended to get him off the hook for not having been a standout among us attack pilots. He knew he would never be recognized for the pilot he thought he was as long as he was stuck in an attack squadron.

It's kind of like not being able to disprove a negative. Since he wasn't in a fighter squadron, we couldn't disprove his assertion about how good he would have been in flying that mission. And that is the way it was until we had been in the squadron for a little over a year.

In the early fall of 1965, the Commandant of the Marine Corps, General Wallace Greene, came to our base and addressed all of the officers on the base regarding the escalating war in South Vietnam. The one statement I still remember is, "If you intend to make a career of the Marine Corps, it is not a matter of whether you go to Vietnam or not, but of how many times you will go."

An A-4 squadron was being formed at our base to go to Vietnam in the early months of the coming year, 1966. When the call went out for volunteers, I quickly put my name on the list, afraid that it would fill up before I could be considered. Most of the other young pilots did the same. But Slick's name was conspicuously absent.

He spent the next few weeks trying to obtain an assignment that would enable him to avoid going to Vietnam. He tried to get orders to the U. S. Naval Training Command as a flight instructor, knowing it would carry him to the end of his obligated term of service. When that failed, I recall hearing that he had tried to obtain an assignment as a general's aide. But that didn't work out, either.

Finally, Marine Corps Headquarters solved the problem in its objective and dispassionate manner, issuing him individual orders to Vietnam as a member of the Marine Air Group at the base where our squadron would be located. Although still unhappy, he felt better than if he had been a member of the newly-formed attack squadron.

On Thanksgiving Day of that year, four couples shared a Thanksgiving meal at one of our homes. I will never forget what Slick said at the table in front of the other pilots and our wives. He knew he would be required to fly at least some combat missions, but felt partially sheltered by being in the Group instead of one of the combat squadrons.

Slick said, "I hope the squadrons have a hard time maintaining their planes so I won't have to fly as many missions." My mouth must have dropped open! How could any red-blooded American serviceman make such a statement about his country's military forces! But I kept my mouth shut and no one else commented either, although I knew the other pilots felt the same way I did.

At the end of February of 1966, our squadron arrived at Chu Lai, Vietnam and our squadron pilots were divided up among the four A-4 squadrons located there. Although Slick had been sent to Vietnam under individual orders to Marine Air Group 12 (MAG -12), he also had been immediately placed in an attack squadron upon arrival.

Slick and I were in separate squadrons, so I lack first-person observations. Maybe he flew as aggressively as all of the other pilots I knew. But I doubt it. An impression had already been formed as far as I was concerned. I recall after a month or so hearing him say something about bombsight settings. He said in conversation with a few other pilots that he had learned to change the bombsight settings to enable him to release his bombs from a higher altitude. This enabled him to pull out of his dive at a higher (and safer) altitude.

Obviously, this would result in less accuracy in the delivery of his bombs. Our bombing attacks were always directed at a certain point on the ground, usually under the direction of an airborne forward air controller. Dropping the bombs from a higher altitude would result in less accuracy. When I mentioned this to Slick, he didn't argue the point and didn't seem to mind.

Consider that you are a Marine on the ground, pinned down by enemy fire and in great need of close air support. Over the horizon comes a flight of A-4's to the rescue. But one of them is piloted by Slick. Are you out of danger yet? Will you ever be out of danger? Does his technique of dropping from a higher altitude pose a greater likelihood of hitting <u>you</u> with his bombs? You know the answers to these questions. The American taxpayers had spent a lot of money training Slick to be an effective attack pilot and he had reneged on performing to the best of his ability.

This story points out the importance of every member of the American team that is associated with a weapon of any type. The weapon has been designed, tested, and manufactured. It is then transported half-way around the world to the combat area and hung upon an airplane. Finally, the pilot delivers the weapon to the best of his ability. Every step in the chain of events is equally important, but the success of the mission can be compromised in the end if the pilot chooses to make an attack with a predictably lower chance of success.

After just a few months into our 12-month tour in Vietnam, the final portion of Slick's combat saga came to an end. He had had the good luck, or foresight, to get into the squadron that would be the next one rotated to Japan for three months. And guess what! When the three months were up, Slick did not return to Vietnam with his squadron-mates! I was told that he had refused to return. Instead, he remained behind at MCAS Iwakuni in an assignment equivalent to serving back in the states.

I still remember when his squadron returned to Chu Lai. Within a few weeks, a young lieutenant in the squadron was killed in an accident during a night combat mission. I remember thinking that it wasn't that it should have been Slick in the accident. But he should at least have been on the line serving his country, sharing the risks as the young lieutenant and others were doing.

My final thought of Slick at the time was that the Marine Corps should have court-martialed him, or any other Marine, for refusing to serve as ordered, in time of war. But even then I realized the intense negative "PR" story this would have entailed for the Marine Corps in mid-1966. I had to just forget the issue and deal with my own missions and concerns about returning home.

Some twenty years later, I spoke with a friend from that era who had become an airline captain, flying Boeing 747's. He brought up the subject of Slick during our conversation, although we didn't dwell on it. He merely mentioned how likable a fellow Slick had been but said he could never understand what had made him behave in the manner in which he had done.

It is actually pretty obvious. Flying military airplanes and living the life of a Marine Corps officer back in the states can be a very rewarding and satisfying experience, as well as a very safe one. One of the greatest of these rewards is knowing that you are in a very enviable position, having attained considerable achievements. Granted that you have made the requisite efforts and sacrifices to get where you are. But the luck of inheriting the right genes and the probable support of your family while growing up also contributed greatly toward your accomplishments.

Another reward is knowing that you are a trained warrior, ready to fight for your country if the situation should arise. But when the bullets begin flying by, or if it appears that they might do so, some people suddenly realize that it is more than they had bargained for. They then may look at the wife and children they love and realize they don't really want to risk losing all they have for their country after all.

And that emotion is understandable, even to the degree that it makes one wonder why so many of our service men and women willingly put themselves into harm's way in the first place. I think it has to begin with love for one's country, to the extent that one is willing to give (or at least risk) his life to defend the ideals for which his country stands. That is what I said about myself sitting on a cot in Vietnam in the summer of 1966, and it was no idle statement. However, by their actions, all of my peers were effectively pledging the same.

A contributing factor promoting brave and unselfish behavior by individuals is their sense of responsibility toward their peers. The respect of these peers is sometimes so important that some individuals have even consciously and willingly given their lives so their friends could survive to fight another day.

I remember the day around August of 1966 when our A-4's were first sent into North Vietnam. It was a four-plane flight and the flight leader was shot down. I remember thinking, "Oh, boy! The first guy that goes up there gets shot down and I still have eight months to go!" You can't help being concerned about your safety and mortality. But when I was placed on the flight schedule for such missions, I flew them and did what I was trained to do without a second thought. And I was only one of thousands that did the same.

Maybe I have been too hard on Slick in my memories of him over the years. It may be asking too much to expect all of our servicemen and servicewomen to be willing to place their lives on the line for their country. Maybe something else is happening. In some cases, the unwillingness may be akin to a mental disorder. We don't expect someone that has a psychological problem (even just to a small degree, but still be able to function) to think or behave like all of the people around them. Perhaps the desire to avoid life-threatening situations is so overpowering that they can do nothing but behave in the self-preserving manner that we observe.

Granted, our young would-be military personnel should realize what they are getting into when they join the military service. But sometimes they may not realize, until the actual risks arrive, that they do not have what it takes to go through with whatever the mission entails.

In simple terms, what is normally considered to be cowardice could possibly be the presence of a psychological condition. I recall reading a story about a Marine Corsair pilot in World War Two. When the squadron went out to fight the Japanese pilots, he always came back with his ammunition expended but his gun camera revealed absolutely nothing. Another pilot decided to follow him on a mission. It turned out that the pilot in question gradually separated himself from the flight. He then flew in large circles until time to return to base. He would then fly into a cloud and expend his ammunition before returning.

After having been exposed, he committed suicide shortly thereafter. He had been unable to bring his problem to the surface and to request release from further participation in combat flying. The resulting shame he experienced following exposure was too much for him to endure, resulting in his ending his own life. (I read this several years ago and it was presented as a true story. However, I have been unable to find it again.)

My discussion here has gone beyond Slick, although he exhibited some of these symptoms, to use that word. To some degree, Slick may well have been a sick man and worthy of sympathy rather than ultimate disrespect. But we had no counselors at Chu Lai. And anyone reporting such concerns is toying with his status as a pilot.

Slick's refusal to return to Vietnam from Japan, although a radical choice akin to the burning of bridges, may have been the only rational choice he could make at the time. Desperate people sometimes take desperate actions.

I have been gracious in giving him the benefit of the doubt. However, another possibility remains in such cases. The individual could simply be saying, "Let the other suckers do it. I'm looking out for number one!"

Who are we to know what went on in the mind of the young man, who only two years before had said, "They call me 'Slick'."

# 17. "YOU 'SHOUDA' BEEN
# IN TH' COCKPIT"

OUR SQUADRON HAD BEEN IN Puerto Rico for only a few days. We were located at the eastern end of the island at a naval air station named Roosevelt Roads. An attack squadron of mostly young lieutenants, we still had a lot to learn but we were gradually becoming more proficient in our A-4 Skyhawks. It was a single-seat, single-engine aircraft and pilots of such planes take no little pride and pleasure in knowing they are the only person in the plane. After a while the plane becomes just an extension of yourself, and its movements become as natural as if you were moving an arm or turning your body in another direction.

Our squadron commander was a slow-talking and quiet-spoken man but he was a salty old aviator who commanded our respect. I say old, but that was only in relative terms, compared to us young pilots in our early and mid-20's. He was old in another way. He had probably been flying jets for the last 20 years and had managed to survive the experience.

We did little flying for the first few days at Rosy Roads, as it was called. Then one night at the club, the colonel and a few others may have stayed at the bar a little later than usual. The next morning, three of us lieutenants showed up at 0630 for our scheduled flight with the colonel. It was going to be an area familiarization flight with some practice formation maneuvers thrown in.

We were the only pilots in the ready room as the colonel commenced briefing the flight. Briefing means that the flight leader goes over the entire plan for the flight, from radio frequencies to a review of the planned maneuvers, and finally setting the fuel state at which "bingo fuel" would be called. The first pilot to get down to this bingo fuel state would call, "Banjo 4, bingo fuel," or whatever. Commencing the return at this time would enable the flight to arrive back at the base with an adequate fuel reserve.

The four pilots sat in a small circle as the colonel began the brief. We lieutenants had our kneeboards on our laps, taking notes as he spoke. However, we found that we had to keep scooting closer and closer to hear his words. He kept speaking lower and lower, sometimes slurring or mumbling the words in some unintelligible manner. It was becoming difficult to understand what the plan of the flight was to be. Finally, the colonel was content with his brief and we stood up to go put on our flight gear. As we left the ready room, he turned to one of the lieutenants and said, "If my plane goes down, you take the flight."

We proceeded to the maintenance area, viewed the records for our planes and walked out on the flight line. Sure enough, as we started our engines and commenced the radio check-in, the colonel radioed that his plane had a problem and for us to go without him. Our substitute flight leader then led us through the flight as best he could until someone finally called bingo fuel. We returned to the base, practiced a few landings and taxied in to the parking area. This was immediately adjacent to what were called the fuel pits, where the planes would be refueled for their next flights.

Because of the expeditionary nature of our visit to Puerto Rico, the squadron's operational facilities were located in large tents at the side of an unused runway on the airfield. As we taxied into the squadron area, the tents housing the squadron were on the opposite side of the runway from the refueling area, where we were to park and shut down the engines.

A ladder was placed against the side of my plane and I commenced stepping out of the cockpit. I was suddenly nearly startled off the ladder by another plane passing very low, fast, and at full power right over our parked planes. I looked up and saw an A-4 commencing an unusually steep climb and the pilot was already dumping his excess fuel as he swirled higher and higher into the sky. He commenced a right turn at an altitude of perhaps four thousand feet and rolled nearly inverted as he began a steep dive back towards the squadron, coming at us from the fuel pits side of the runway.

By now I was standing on the ground as I saw his plane plummeting downward in a near vertical dive. Then the nose gradually began to rise. I had never seen anything like it and never would again. I said to the pilot beside me, "He'll never make it!" His airplane was laboring to pull out and it was truly nip and tuck as to whether he would clear the ground or not. Miraculously, he barely missed hitting the ground as he flew directly over the large rubber fuel bags while coming straight toward us. He cleared the fueling area, the airplanes, and the entire squadron behind us by only tens of feet as he roared overhead.

Several minutes later the colonel came taxiing into the squadron area, parked his plane and stepped from the cockpit. He was met by perhaps a dozen wide-eyed young lieutenants. Someone said, "Damn, colonel! You really scared us!" The colonel cocked his head slightly to one side and slowly and quietly said, "You shoulda' been in th' cockpit."

Our commanding officer had come within a hair of wiping out the entire squadron. It was close!

# 18. TWO HUNDRED FEET
# AT SIX O'CLOCK

I FLEW 5,600 HOURS IN about a dozen different kinds of aircraft during my 20-year Marine Corps career, with about 1,500 of them being in tactical (combat) aircraft. The combat plane that I flew the most was the A-4 Skyhawk. It was considered to be a small plane and had only one engine. Nearly all of my 250 combat missions in Vietnam were flown in the single-seat version of this plane. I eventually accumulated over 1,100 flight hours in this aircraft and, like all of the pilots that ever flew it, loved every minute of it. Well, almost every minute.

Surprisingly, the plane had a nuclear delivery capability and I once read that this was the mission it had been designed for in the first place. It was one of the first planes the U. S. Navy had that could launch from the carriers on a nuclear bombing mission. The Marine squadrons also maintained this capability throughout the cold war with their A-4 squadrons.

All of the pilots in the squadron were trained to fly the nuclear delivery maneuvers. Later, however, only three or four received the full ground school training for these missions. And, during the year and a half that I was in the squadron, Todd Eikenberry (another first lieutenant) and I were the only pilots to fly a complete simulated nuclear delivery mission. All of the squadron pilots qualified for the Military Occupational Specialty (MOS) of 7501, Basic Attack Pilot. But only Todd and I and maybe another pilot or two achieved the secondary MOS of 7592, Nuclear Delivery Pilot.

This was obviously a significant qualification. If the international situation had ever deteriorated to the extent that commencement of a major war became imminent, pilots having this qualification would have been moved into positions around the world from which nuclear attacks would have been launched upon the enemy, hopefully preemptively. Later, during my first tour in Vietnam in 1966, I flew to Japan for one week of refresher training in nuclear weapons delivery, including flights where the required special delivery techniques were practiced. In this case, it was a good deal to get out of Vietnam for a week, plus an opportunity to visit Japan as well.

If we had ever been launched on a nuclear bombing mission, it would have been a flight over a long distance. A tanker plane would therefore have accompanied us, perhaps even another A-4, carrying an extra fuel tank for us to draw fuel from via in-flight refueling. That was very difficult to do at night, by the way!

After topping off our tanks at some point, the tanker would return to base (lucky guy) while we delivery pilots would have continued on to our targets. Finally, at some point, we would have descended to minimum altitude (perhaps 100 feet off the treetops) to go in under the radar. Eventually we would accelerate to arrive at our initial point (IP) at 500 knots, and be on our final heading toward the target.

We would have double-checked all of the armament switches as we approached the target. Flying directly over its center, we would begin a four and one-half "g" pull-up into what would have appeared to have been the commencement of a loop. After passing approximately thirty degrees past straight up, the bomb would have been automatically released as we continued the apparent loop through the inverted position. Continuing down the back side of the loop, we would have rolled the plane back upright and pulled out at the planned burst altitude of the weapon. We would have been at full power trying to get the hell out of there back the way we had come before the bomb went off!

The bomb would have been pre-set for either an air-burst or a surface burst, depending upon the nature of the target. We were told that when the blast effects caught up with us, the plane would have been nearly destroyed by the intense heat and wind effects. We would have been wearing an asbestos flight suit, special gloves, oxygen mask, and helmet. Finally, special heat shields would have been pulled forward around the inside of the canopy. But we would still have been lucky to have survived.

They told us that if we did make it back to our base, our planes would probably never fly again. And we may have just killed a million people. But like General Sherman said, "War is hell."

After being in the squadron for about a year, Todd and I were scheduled for our simulated nuclear missions. This was a big thing because we were representing the squadron, competing with all of the other Marine A-4 squadrons in what were called Competitive Exercises (Compexes).

One afternoon we were assigned targets for our missions and told the exact times our bombs were to hit the target the next day. We were to plan the entire missions as though they were the real thing. We had to calculate the bomb settings and plan every step of the flight including fuel consumption along the way. A check pilot (Captain Gordon Booth, from the staff of Marine Air Group 14) would quiz us on all required knowledge before going to the plane. Finally, Captain Booth would fly the chase plane to grade us on how well we flew our routes and would grade the accuracy of our bomb delivery on the targets.

The next day Todd and I launched separately on our individual missions. The planes were at their maximum takeoff weight, carrying two 2,000-lb fuel tanks and a 2,000-lb simulated nuclear weapon. During takeoff, Todd's nose tire blew out at nearly takeoff speed. He responded perfectly, however, successfully aborting the takeoff by shutting down the engine, dropping his arresting hook and being stopped by the arresting gear at the end of the runway.

My takeoff was normal and the flight went well until I was in the pull-up over the target and the bomb failed to release. Upon return to the base it was found to have been caused by a faulty electrical circuit and I would have to make another flight just to drop the bomb. This time, it consisted of just the run-in to the target at 500 knots and 100 feet of altitude and dropping the practice bomb. However, a bad combination of crosswind and headwind existed at the target that could have possibly prevented me from qualifying. The qualifying score was to hit within 700 feet of the target. A hit within 400 feet would give me the maximum score.

I compensated for the wind by flying a few hundred feet to the left of the target and delayed the pull-up into the attack maneuver by what I thought was an adequate amount. I held the four and one-half g's as the plane climbed toward the sky. Shortly after passing through the vertical, the bomb released properly this time. It soared up to an altitude of around 13,000 feet while my plane topped out at about 8,000 feet going over the top of the maneuver. Many seconds later, my chase pilot Gordon Booth and I saw the splash of the bomb hit, nearly two miles below. He said over the radio, "Two hundred feet at 6 o'clock."

For my accomplishment I received a large, impressive document signed by the Commanding General of the Second Marine Aircraft Wing, General A. L. Bowser. A large "E" was in the background of the text of the document. Frankly, I never paid much attention to it over the years. I learned much later that this E was a very significant award. I quote, "The 'E' is the highest service award the Navy can make and it means excellence or special merit in gunnery, engineering or other activity." In my case, it was for successful completion of the simulated nuclear delivery mission and the overall attainment of combat readiness that it represented. A copy of the award is at the appendix.

I was one of the relatively few single-seater pilots that would have ever been called upon to deliver a nuclear weapon. Granted, it may have been a dubious honor, but to us Marine and Navy pilots, that is what we were there for.

So, in my case, it was "Am qualified, will deliver!"

# 19. CLIMBING THROUGH THIRTY FEET

WELL, WHAT'S THE BIG DEAL about climbing through thirty feet? You do it on every flight, don't you? Yes, you do, unless it is going to be a very unusual flight where you spend a lot of time very close to the ground.

In this case, I'm not talking about the moments right after takeoff. It was an hour into the flight and I was making 500 knots right down on the deck, as we would say. To put it into perspective, that is about 850 feet per second. And I happen to remember that the muzzle velocity of a Colt .45 automatic pistol is 905 feet per second!

It was the summer of 1965 and I was flying a training mission out of Marine Corps Air Station (MCAS) Cherry Point, North Carolina in an A-4E Skyhawk. The target was BT-9, an old sunken ship protruding from the water in a bay on the Atlantic coast. BT-9 meant Bombing Target # 9.

I was running in on a practice maneuver, all alone in my single-seater A-4 Skyhawk. We pilots liked flying that way. But it comes with a price. Sometimes it would help to have another pair of eyes to be of assistance, in a lot of ways. I never flew fighter combat missions but I know having that extra pair of eyes might make the difference between success and failure in a dogfight, and could easily mean the difference between life and death.

The practice attack maneuver consisted of running in at 500 knots at one hundred feet above the surface of the water. At around two miles or so from the target, we would begin a four and one-half "g" pullup until the plane was about sixty degrees nose up. We would then roll to inverted flight and bring the nose back down to the target, still inverted. Rolling back upright, we would then make whatever attack was planned.

The purpose of the low-altitude approach was to minimize the possibility of visual detection by the target. The high speed was to minimize the time approaching the target and also to provide the necessary energy to execute the pullup for the attack.

The A-4 had an on-board radar, the APG-53A, which I was using to determine my pullup point. Something to know about radar, however, is that the closer you get to the target, the greater the return on the screen. The pilot therefore had to frequently reduce the power of the radar by turning the gain knob down. A slight problem, however, is that this necessitated looking back into the cockpit to adjust the return on the screen, after locating the small knob by the radar screen.

Regarding the altitude, the plane had a radar altimeter which displayed the altitude of the plane using a logarithmic scale. It wasn't particularly accurate at higher altitudes, but below 100 feet, the graduations were larger-spaced, enabling the exact altitude of the plane to be read. It contained a small, red warning light that would illuminate when the aircraft descended below a preset altitude, 100 feet in this case.

So there I was, booming along at 500 knots and 100 feet, occasionally adjusting the gain on the radar as I closed on the target. But one time, while making this adjustment, I suddenly realized that my head had been in the cockpit a little too long. I quickly looked up and through the windscreen. I was about to hit the water! I quickly pulled up and as the nose came up through the horizon, I instinctively glanced at the radar altimeter down at the bottom right corner of the instrument panel. I was climbing through thirty feet!

How low did I go? I don't know. I once saw a pilot (Bill Gash) ahead of me in a strafing run at this same target go so low that I saw the water spread underneath his plane as he pulled out. And our squadron later lost another pilot and plane at nearby BT-11, flying at the same altitude and airspeed.

A plane from another squadron hit the water under similar circumstances while I was at Cherry Point and both crewmembers ejected safely. And in 1966 my best friend, Norm Bundy, was killed in an F-8 Crusader while flying a high-speed photo reconnaissance mission over North Vietnam. He hit the ground at over 500 knots. His head was probably in the cockpit as he was setting up the switches for the cameras as he approached the target area.

It was one of the occupational hazards that we faced. Looking back on it, I could have run in at 200 feet and no one would have known the difference. But there is the principle of training like you fight. If you don't train properly, you may not be able to perform adequately when it is done for real.

I never flew that maneuver in combat, but in all of my combat missions, I felt ready in every attack run I ever made because I had paid the price in training. And with a lot of luck and perhaps some poor shooting on some people's part on the ground, I was able to return home safely. And I thank God for that.

# 20. "REMEMBER TO PULL OUT"

IT WAS THE SUMMER OF 1966 and I had been flying combat missions in the A-4 Skyhawk for the past five months, both night and day. Besides dropping bombs and firing rockets, the plane also had two 20-mm cannons, one at each wing root. They weren't cannons in the usual sense of the word. Twenty millimeters is about 0.8 of an inch and apparently there is some dividing line at which they are no longer called machine guns but cannons, instead. For all practical purposes, they were 20-mm machine guns but we just called them guns.

There were two gun switches at the left side of the instrument panel, marked left and right, for their respective guns. These switches armed the guns from a compressed air bottle in the right wheel well where the right landing gear is stowed in flight. I always liked the experience of charging the guns upon arrival in the target area. It made a "ka-fump" feeling, shaking the entire plane slightly as the rounds were rammed into the firing chambers. There was something nearly sensual about it and you always felt like you were now really loaded for bear.

After expending our bombs or rockets, we would often be called upon to strafe the target area with our guns. Firing the guns and firing rockets were similar in a deadly way. I say deadly meaning potentially deadly to the pilot. The problem was that when either one was fired, there was the natural desire to watch the bullets or rockets as they sped ahead on their way to the target.

If you didn't pull out in time while firing rockets, you could possibly fly through the fragmentation pattern. Those are big words that mean you might be hit by the fragments exploding up into your flight path. The proper procedure was to pull the trigger and begin an immediate pullout.

There was no point in watching the rockets. You had no further control of them.

Firing the guns was a different problem. We normally fired about a two to three-second burst. But even in that small amount of time, we could see the rounds begin to impact the target. There was a natural reaction to want to control the stream of rounds, that is, to direct them as you would with a hose. The only problem was that you were diving toward the ground at over 500 miles per hour! It was such a common occurrence that it had long been given a name. It was called target fixation.

*LtCol. Jack Harris, Lieutenants Jim Hartmann and Leo Holler over the Ho Chi Minh Trail in 1966. Photo by the author.*

One of our pilots had struck the treetops while strafing before I joined the squadron. He managed to bring the plane back but it never flew again. Another good friend also flew through some treetops during a low pullout but managed to keep the plane airborne. Unfortunately, his engine quit and he had to eject. He was killed during the rescue attempt when he fell from a rope lowered to him by a crewman on an Army helicopter. The rope had a loop in the end of it. If he had gotten into the loop, he would have been saved. But in the intense heat of the moment, he merely held onto the rope and then fell off due to the high wind blast as the helicopter sped away from the enemy fire.

I don't remember the particulars of the first time I nearly hit the trees. I just remember it was over the Ho Chi Minh Trail in Laos and we were strafing the target area after expending all of our bombs on trucks under the trees. I particularly remember the momentary fright as I pulled out at absolute tree-top level. I felt like I had green all around me at my lowest point in the pullout. I remember being so concerned that after landing I looked on the underside of the airplane to see if there were any green stains. There were none, through no fault of my own!

The second time was much more memorable. Another pilot and I had just completed the bombing portion of yet another mission over the Ho Chi Minh Trail when we spotted a truck on a dirt road on a hillside. We decided to attack it with our guns. Unfortunately, a low overcast prevented us from making a diving attack so our right-hand circular attack pattern was made nearly level toward the truck, being located about halfway up the hillside.

*LtCol Jack Harris, (CO, VMA-311), Lieutenants Jim Hartmann and Leo Holler. Photo by the author.*

I still remember the right turn at over 400 knots with my left wingtip seemingly in the bottom of the overcast. I kept the turn going as I drew the nose of the plane around toward the truck. I pulled the gunsight onto the truck and began firing even before my wings were level and began walking the rounds into the truck. Then I was level and the rounds were hitting it as I hurtled toward the hillside. Nearly too late! I quickly pulled up and over the ridgeline, actually feeling a burble of air as the wind passed over the hill. I had been lucky! It was terribly close.

I told myself that henceforth, whenever I began a rocket or gun attack, I would always remind myself before every run, "Remember to pullout!" And I did.

# 21. "SAM SITE" IN THE DMZ

IT WAS THE SUMMER OF 1966 and I was a squadron pilot in VMA-311 at Chu Lai, Vietnam. Another pilot and I had just returned from a mission and we were being debriefed at the Marine Air Group headquarters as per usual. Suddenly, another officer burst in and said that a SAM site (Surface to Air Missile) had reportedly been seen in the DMZ area between South and North Vietnam.

The SAM missiles were radar-guided and could easily home in on aircraft once their controlling radar locked on to them. They were quite large missiles, perhaps 40 to 50 feet in length, each carrying a powerful explosive warhead. The presence of such weapons in the DMZ area would have presented an intolerable situation for our aviation forces.

No SAM sites had ever been detected in the DMZ, Laos, or in South Vietnam. Built and supplied by the Soviet Union, they were often manned or administered by Soviet advisors. Wiping these advisors out along with the SAM site would not have bothered me in the least. We were in a very local war against communism there in Vietnam. But there was a much larger Cold War that had been in effect since 1945 and would continue for another twenty-three years.

President Reagan would later correctly describe the Soviet Union as an evil empire. I didn't need to be told that, although the man in the street probably did. As far as I was concerned, a communist was a communist and I would have blown them all away. Anyone having a problem with that attitude did not understand the true nature of the threat that communism posed to mankind.

I couldn't have cared less what economic model Russia or any other nation chose to follow. The problem was communism's stated goal of ultimate world conquest and domination. I hasten to add that only a very small percent of the population of the communist nations were communists. It is to that group of people that I direct these comments.

But right then I had to deal with immediate issues. My wingman and I were ordered to fly to the DMZ, find the SAM site and destroy it. That is sort of like telling you to go out into the woods, find a rattlesnake, and then kill it with a small stick. The biggest problem in the assignment was that the mission of SAM sites was to shoot down airplanes!

An additional problem was that the SAM sites were always heavily defended by regular anti-aircraft weapons. If a SAM site had truly existed in the area, this would have been such a dangerous mission that we would have been lucky to have returned safely to our base.

Two aircraft were hurriedly armed with the new Mark-4 gunpods that had recently arrived at the base. These gunpods were about the same size as our 2,000-lb drop tanks and were capable of a very high rate of fire of 20-mm cannon rounds. With these weapons we would really be able to destroy the site if we could get it in our gunsights. Our last instruction was that if we failed to find the SAM site, we were to fly out over the water and exercise the guns on the way back to the base.

I don't remember who led the flight. Upon arrival at the DMZ, we stayed below 2,000 feet of altitude and could see the area well but never observed anything resembling a SAM site. We flew low and fast, back and forth over the suspected area, with the wingman trailing the leader by a few thousand feet. We both kept changing our directions to minimize the possibility of being hit by ground fire . If the leader had been fired upon by a missile, presumably the wingman would have see the origin of the missile's launch and been able to attack it.

Finally, we left the DMZ, flew eastward out over the water and turned south for the flight back toward home. Remembering our final instructions, we armed our gunpods and pulled the triggers. Neither one of my gunpods fired and only one of his did! We still had our regular 20-mm guns, but we would have been at a distinct disadvantage not having the heavy firepower of the gunpods. Still, I would loved to have hosed it down, if just with my regular 20-millimeter guns!

## 22. THE DAY I WAS SCARED

It was a hot afternoon at Chu Lai in June of 1966. I had been flying combat missions daily in the A-4 Skyhawk since arriving in Vietnam three months earlier. On this day our squadron had the hot pad duty. Instead of flying regularly scheduled missions, we had planes and crews at the ready for any emergency missions that might arise.

Six planes were fueled, loaded, preflighted, and awaited their pilots to climb in, start their engines, and head off to goodness knows where. Two planes each carried ten 250-pound regular bombs which would be dropped during our dive bombing runs. We normally released them two at a time from an altitude of 3000 feet at a speed of 450 knots. We would then pull out at 4 1/2 g's, clearing the target by around 1,500 feet of elevation. Two other planes were loaded with "guns and rockets." The rockets were 5-inch "Zuni" rockets, four under each wing. The guns were actually gun pods, one under each wing. Each gun could fire dozens of 20-mm rounds per second for perhaps 10 seconds of firing time. We were told to limit our firing bursts to one and half seconds to avoid damaging the barrels. One of our pilots once broke that rule and ruined the barrels on both of his gun pods.

The last two were loaded with what were called "Snake-eyes." These bombs had devices attached at the rear that would spread after release from the plane. This slowed the bomb's speed, enabling the plane to release at a much lower altitude and still be clear of the bomb's fragmentation pattern as it sped on past the target.

Dropping the bombs at a point much closer to the target enabled us to achieve much greater accuracy. The Snake-eyes were dropped at 450 knots in a ten-degree dive. The plane would then clear the target by only

100 feet of elevation during the pullout. There was little room for error with Snake-eyes.

Six pilots sat in a building similar to our new hootches, about two hundred feet away from the planes. Four lounged in their flight suits while the other two sat sweating in full flight gear, ready to run toward the planes on a moment's notice. I was one of these pilots when the phone rang. The responder turned and called, "Snake-eyes!" and my flight leader Butch Miller and I ran for the planes.

We were airborne in a matter of minutes, booming southward down the coast at 400 knots. Butch called the airborne "FAC" (Forward Air Controller) as we neared the target area and we were briefed on the mission. An American army unit was pinned down by heavy fire and had already taken casualties. Our mission was to take out the enemy who was separated from the friendlies by only 100 meters. That raised concern because of the danger of hitting our own troops.

Normally, the airborne FAC would mark the target with a smoke rocket to show us where to commence bombing. We would not have this luxury today as he said the ground fire was so intense he couldn't get near the target. I thought to myself, "Oh, boy. He can't even get near the target and I've got to pull out directly over their guns at 100 feet!"

Butch informed him that we had ten 250 pounders each. The FAC asked him how he wanted to drop his bombs and Butch replied, "We'll drop two bombs per pass." That was gutsy! He could have said we would drop them all at once. That would have minimized our exposure but if we missed the target our effort would have been wasted and the friendlies would still be under fire.

Butch fishtailed his plane, signaling me to separate for our individual attacks. He then rolled in from about two thousand feet, commencing his first run. And that is when it happened. In some 250 combat missions, many of them encountering ground fire, this was the only moment I ever felt fear. And it lasted at least three seconds. Okay, maybe only two. After all, within the next minute I could be ejecting from a shot-up airplane, or worse, be part of the wreckage in the target area.

The gunners on the ground were about to have a clear shot at an A-4 diving straight at them, pulling out at only 100 feet over their heads. I didn't dwell on it but concentrated on what I had to do. As I rolled in, the FAC said, "Move your bombs twenty meters to the left of his hit." Approaching the target, I saw the ground fire commence and the yellow tracers began flashing past the cockpit. I released two snake-eyes and pulled out, banking left in a climbing turn as Butch rolled in on his next run. The momentary fear was gone.

Now we settled into our routine attack procedures. We continued our runs, covering the target area in response to the FAC's directions. After expending our bombs we strafed the area with our 20-mm guns. When we were done, the FAC reported that the ground commander said they were no longer being fired upon. I joined back up on Butch and we flew more leisurely back toward home, completing what was to become one of my most memorable combat missions.

# 23. A MOMENT IN TIME

I READ YEARS AGO THAT when we remember something from the past, we remember moments, not days. A more important point is that there are <u>critical</u> moments in our lives, but we usually do not recognize their significance at the time. However, they occur in all of our lives. I define a critical moment as a moment in which some life-changing event either occurs, or could possibly occur, depending upon our reaction to the event.

I've included in my stories how some of these moments have occurred in my life over the years. There was the time that, because a parking place was closer to one corner than the next, I ended up in the Marine Corps instead of the Air Force. On another occasion, I chose to make an extreme effort to finish in first place in a physical fitness test while in Preflight training.

This resulted in an apparent overstress of my kidneys and I was held back for over three months while the doctors figured out what to do with me. Because of this medical hold, I was later returned to training with an entirely different set of flight students. And, in fact, I met my future wife through one of these students. A critical moment on an afternoon of routine physical training had rolled an entirely different set of dice for my entire future life.

There was the critical moment when my head had been in the cockpit for a little too long and I nearly hit the water at 500 knots! There were others in Vietnam when I nearly hit the trees while strafing ground targets. And there was the time I edged just a little further up an earthen bank and, fewer than ten seconds later, a 20-mm round missed me by inches, striking the man next to me instead.

Yes, there have been many critical moments in my life, just as there have been for everyone. The only difference is that some of mine may have been a little more dramatic.

Time spent in combat situations is filled with critical moments, usually passing unnoticed or at least not commented upon. There are the zipping sounds of bullets passing close enough by to be heard. And there are mortar rounds that hit just far enough away to not have changed or ended your life. And goodness knows how many rounds went flying past my plane during my bombing, rocket, and strafing runs while accumulating some 250 combat missions.

The first black Naval Aviator, Ensign Jesse Brown of Hattiesburg, Mississippi, was a victim of such a moment over North Korea in December of 1950. Struck by anti-aircraft fire during an attack run, the engine of his gull-winged F4U Corsair quit while returning to his aircraft carrier, following loss of oil pressure. Ensign Brown was forced to make a crash landing into mountainous terrain with the end result being the loss of his life. A critical moment had existed when at least one if not many bullets had struck his plane.

On an early morning flight in Vietnam in the summer of 1966, Bill Hawking, a squadron-mate, encountered his critical moment as his plane struck the trees during a low pullout. Although he survived the ejection from the damaged plane, he was killed during the ensuing rescue attempt by helicopter.

Being rushed by the approach of enemy soldiers, he hurriedly clung to a rope that was dropped from an army helicopter, instead of climbing into the loop that it presented. A speed of 100 knots is not fast by aircraft standards, but it was more than Bill could do to hang on as the helicopter left the rescue area under enemy fire.

We lost a pilot in another squadron that I was flying with in 1970. He and another pilot were flying a two-seater version of the A-4 Skyhawk. During the course of the mission, only one bullet struck the plane. Unfortunately, it struck the pilot in the front seat in the head, killing him instantly. The pilot in the rear cockpit was able to return the plane to base successfully.

One of my best friends during pre-flight training was Dave Carver, a young Marine lieutenant like me. His grades in primary flight training were not quite high enough for jets so he went through basic training in the prop-driven T-28. He must have done well, however, because the next time I saw him was in Vietnam, where we often flew together in the same A-4 squadron.

*The author with Dave Carver at Chu Lai in 1966*

During one of Dave's missions, a bullet passed through his cockpit literally inches in front of his face. He was pulling out at over 500 mph when the bullet came through the left side of his canopy and exited the right side. If Dave's plane had been just inches further ahead in its attack run, he would have been immediately killed. If the round had been fired one thousandth of a second later, he also would have been killed. Dave was indeed lucky to have lived through his critical moment.

It was a matter of mathematical odds. If the enemy gunners could fire enough rounds out in front of an attacking plane, one would eventually strike it and possibly bring it down. Similarly, the more missions a pilot flew, the greater was the likelihood that his plane would eventually be hit.

Despite these obvious facts, the pilots wanted to fly the missions. It is a credit to the professionalism and aggressiveness of our pilots, and their willingness to risk their all for their country, that they approached their combat missions eagerly and with enthusiasm. I am truly fortunate and proud to have been a member of this elite group of young men who served their country in this manner.

# 24. "I'M REALLY TIRED TONIGHT"

JUST EVERYDAY LIFE AT CHU LAI was fatiguing in that spring and summer of 1966. For that matter, it was still fatiguing in the fall of 1969 when I returned for my second year in Vietnam, again flying A-4's out of Chu Lai. The base was located right on the beach and the sands penetrated inland past the confines of the airbase, including the runway. A small ridge of sand paralleled the beach a few hundred feet in from the shore. All of the living quarters and associated buildings were on the seaward side of this ridge. The flight line and runway were on the other (western) side of this ridge, also paralleling the shore.

What contributed so much to the fatigue was the ubiquitous sand. It was everywhere. As time passed, wooden pallets were gradually scrounged to serve as walkways between the tents and buildings. In the heat of the day, the sand reflected the heat upon your body as you trudged along. We pilots normally lived in our dark green flight suits which further absorbed the heat of the sun and sand.

Air conditioning didn't exist, of course, and we initially lived in large green tents which really soaked up the sun's heat. There was little to no shade. I don't mean to complain. I'm just describing the environment. Within a few months the tents had been replaced by what were called hootches. These were just raised floors covered by tin roofs. But they were really cool compared to the tents previously used.

Another contributing factor towards fatigue was the nearly ever-present sound of the jet engines. The flight line faced towards the beach and our working areas. The A-4 was considered to be a small jet as combat planes went. But even at idle rpm it produced a very loud and shrill sound that was projected forward with great intensity. After starting the engines for a mission, it always took several minutes to go through all of the post-start checks before finally taxiing from the flight line to the runway for takeoff.

*The author with tents and sand at Chu Lai in 1966*

We flew at least once every day and flying two flights per day was not unusual. Occasionally a few of the pilots were selected to fly a third mission on a given day. Don't get me wrong. We pilots loved to fly and flying real combat missions was the best flying that we ever did. And we wanted to fly them. As I've written elsewhere, it was, "Why does he have two flights and I only have one?" Or, "Why does he have three flights and I only have two?" However, flying the missions increased the fatigue level when combined with the overall conditions in our living and work environment.

The summertime heat was always a factor during day operations. Take a look at the pictures of jet pilots sometime and look at all of the stuff we had to wear. There were the green Nomex flight suits and high-top flight boots. A g-suit was worn covering the abdomen, thighs and calves. A torso harness was worn to provide a foundation for strapping one's body into the ejection seat. A survival kit was worn around the chest, complete with "Mae West" flotation device, pistol, survival knife, and flare gun. Flight gloves and helmet rounded out the attire, with the oxygen mask pressed against your face after fastening it to each side of the helmet.

By the time we were strapped into the planes, we could already feel sweat trickling down our backs. After starting the engine, the canopy was lowered and the air conditioning was turned on. Don't shout for joy yet! At idle engine speed the air conditioning didn't put out enough cooling for the cockpit. Unfortunately, the canopy still had to be in the closed position to cool the electronic equipment. The cockpit itself was not cooled until the engine rpm was increased for takeoff. It worked fine when airborne. But once back on the ground we were again stuck under a hot canopy with the sun's rays beaming through onto us with no air conditioning.

After landing we had to taxi into the fuel pits where the plane was pressure-fueled through the refueling probe. We had to sit there with the engine running until the refueling operation was completed. One pilot took a thermometer along one hot day and reported that the cockpit temperature was 135 degrees during the refueling operation. Finally, upon returning to the flight line, we were able to shut down the engine and raise the canopy. It sure felt good to get out of the plane and get the flight gear back off and go to Group Headquarters for a mission debrief. Then if we were lucky, we got to go do it all over again a couple of hours later!

On some good days, you got to fly three flights! I emphasize yet again that getting to fly the combat missions was what we wanted to do. I know that is counter-intuitive to non-pilot ears, which means it doesn't make good sense. But I've read books about combat flying in WW I, WW II, and Korea since I was a teenager and all of the great fighter pilots craved going on the missions. I don't mean to elevate ourselves to that "great" status, but at least we fulfilled that portion of the definition.

However, there was a downside. In addition to the fatigue induced by the environmental conditions, there was sometimes some degree of stress from the missions themselves. So, by the third flight of the day, one could obviously be tired. And after all, what we were doing did not give us the luxury of mistakes. An extra blink of the eye or minor distraction here or there could result in hitting the trees. Or a low pullout or failing to pull out in time could result in flying through one's own bomb or rocket fragmentation pattern.

I remember night flights over the Ho Chi Minh trail in Laos during that summer. The trail was a network of dirt roads running primarily north to south down the eastern edge of Laos, bordering South Vietnam. The presence of our daytime bombing flights prevented their use for resupply during the day so they resorted to trucking their provisions during the night hours. To cause them problems and attempt to destroy trucks, supplies, and hopefully their personnel too, we would send flights of two A-4's to conduct night dive-bombing attacks.

We would meet up with a C-130 out of one of the Air Force bases in Thailand. After they detected movement of trucks, perhaps by radar, they would mark the targets by some kind of flare for our bombing attacks. Now that will scare the hell out of you! Diving toward the dark ground at night is certainly a dangerous undertaking. From a pure piloting viewpoint, however, it was not only challenging, requiring great concentration, but also fun as well in its own way.

An equally dangerous portion of these flights was just flying formation on your flight leader prior to separating for our individual attack runs. We would be at about seven or eight thousand feet of altitude with our external lights turned off to keep from being seen by the enemy gunners. That wasn't a problem for the flight leader but it sure was for the wingman. I don't recall ever having the luxury of any appreciable moonlight for assistance during these missions. All I can remember is how dark it was and how difficult it was to fly in formation near the leader.

Flying formation requires the ability to sense what we pilots call relative motion between yourself and your leader. Under conditions of darkness you could suddenly find yourself moving dangerously close to his plane. That spurred a quick reaction of reducing the power and initiating enough of a turn away to keep from running into his plane.

On one dark night, we lost one of our squadron pilots, Jim Villeponteaux, on one of these missions over Laos. With a name like that, we generally just referred to him as "V-13." We had a "W-11" also, in Ed Weihenmayer. Jim was flying his third flight of the day as a wingman to Connie Silard, who seemed to have picked up the nickname Motormouth. He was a good pilot, though, and a sound flight leader. On this flight, he and Jim had turned off their lights as described previously but had not yet separated for their individual bombing runs.

Connie later said he felt a solid bump on the underside of his plane while in a turn. He tried to call Jim but received no response. Many seconds later a fireball was observed in the dark jungle a mile and a half below. Jim had apparently fallen victim to the difficult task of flying night formation on an airplane with its lights turned off. The impact with Connie's plane probably involved the canopy area of Jim's plane and he may have been incapacitated by the impact. All of us that had flown such missions could understand how it had occurred.

The rest of us pilots didn't learn about it until the next day as we had gone to bed before Connie returned with the bad news. This was a particularly sad loss because I knew that Jim had a pretty and devoted wife and several small children. Jim was a very good-natured young pilot and was well-liked by all.

When a pilot was being strapped into his plane, a plane captain was there to assist him. The plane captain was a young enlisted man who was assigned to the flight line to service the plane and pre-flight it before arrival of the pilot. After assisting the pilot in getting strapped in to the ejection seat, he observed the engine start and assisted with the post-start checks of the plane. Later, he removed the landing gear safety pins upon signal by the pilot. Finally, he pulled the wheel chocks when directed, and sent the plane on its way when the pilot was ready to taxi to the runway.

The next day, the plane captain told of helping Jim get strapped in for what was to be his last flight. Jim was serving his country that day and night, half a world away from his beloved wife and kids. He had already flown two combat flights and was being strapped in for the third time that day, a Marine willingly doing his duty as he had been trained to do. As the plane captain completed his assistance, helping Jim get strapped into the cockpit, Jim had turned to him and said, "I'm really tired tonight."

I wish Jim had flown only two flights that day.

# 25. THE OFFICIAL OPENING
# OF RUNWAY 31 RIGHT

NEXT TO HAVING AN AIRCRAFT that works, i.e., the engine runs and all of the mechanical systems function normally, the most important requirements are to have navigational and communication (radio) equipment that function properly. The navigational equipment is there to enable the pilot to get the plane from point A to point B, and is absolutely essential under conditions of adverse weather. The radio is required for air-to-ground and air-to-air communication.

I have read that in the early months of the Second World War, some of the Japanese fighter planes were in combat situations without radios. They would have been at a great disadvantage in not being able to be warned of enemy aircraft commencing an attack upon them. This condition was probably rectified quite quickly.

In the years that I flew, the aircraft were equipped with only one UHF radio, usually the ARC-27, although other models were used later. Granted, the radios were very reliable, but they still failed at times. Usually, flights of tactical aircraft contained at least two planes. This provided a safety factor as it was unlikely that two or more planes would lose their radios during the same flight.

Whenever one of the aircraft lost a radio, the pilot of the other plane would become the flight leader. Upon return to the field, the new wingman (sans radio) would fly on the leader's wing as the flight made a straight-in approach to the runway. The leader would signal when to drop the landing gear and flaps and both planes would execute this at exactly the same time. Since the planes normally were of the same type, the aerodynamic reactions affected both planes in the same manner, and the wingman could maintain his position of formation.

If this occurred under instrument flight conditions, it was more difficult for the wingman, and if it happened at night, the problem was magnified even further. But the pilots were expected to accomplish these requirements and they normally did so successfully.

One friend, and an ex-flight student of mine to boot, was Jot Eve. Jot lost his life in the western Pacific in the mid-1970's, I don't know where, when going through this flight transition under adverse conditions. One of the planes had lost its radio and the other pilot was trying to lead the stricken plane back to the aircraft carrier.

To make it worse, the planes were not of the same type and they reacted differently to the changing aerodynamic loads as their landing gear and flaps were lowered. Finally, it was my understanding that the accident occurred at night, thereby presenting the entire worst case scenario. The two aircraft ran together at some point and both were lost, including the flight crews as well.

In Vietnam it was not uncommon for one of the planes to occasionally lose its radio. I remember times being led back to the field and on occasion being the leader that returned the wingman. After lowering the gear and flaps, we would continue descending toward the duty runway. All of this time, the wingman would have been concentrating on flying formation on his leader.

When cleared to land, the leader would pat the dashboard of his cockpit, point to the runway, and give a thumbs-up signal to his wingman. This indicated to the wingman that he was cleared to land and to take over on his own for the remainder of the landing.

During the summer of 1966, this seemingly straight-forward practice once went awry at our air base. It involved two aircraft from our squadron, VMA-311. I don't remember who the leader was, but the wingman was Lieutenant Colonel Joe Pultorak. I believe Colonel Pultorak was assigned to the Group instead of one of the four squadrons. However, Group pilots flew their share of missions as well. Another factor was that Colonel Pultorak was rather new at the base and not quite as familiar with the airfield.

A short discussion of airfields is required to fully appreciate what transpired next during the landing in question. Some airfields have so much air traffic that they utilize parallel runways, thereby enabling takeoffs and landings to be conducted simultaneously. If the runways are oriented north and south, for example, they are called Runway 36 Left and Runway 36 Right. The "36" is a sort of shorthand, indicating that the heading of the runway is approximately 360 degrees if viewed from the south.

Our field consisted primarily of a single 8,000-foot runway for normal use. A shorter crosswind runway also existed at the north end of the field but does not enter into this story. I recall that the runway was 102 feet wide, which was fairly narrow for the use it received. The fact that it was narrow affected the event in question.

An even narrower, parallel taxiway ran the length of the runway, being positioned perhaps 200 feet to the east, toward the seaward side of the field. The northern one-third of the taxiway was home to the four A-4 squadrons. For protection against mortar attacks, walls consisting of 55-gallon barrels of sand were placed between each pair of airplanes. The southern-most squadron was VMA-224.

The scene was set as described as the flight of two A-4 Skyhawks approached the runway from the south. The leader had set-up his wingman, Colonel Pultorak, to land on Runway 31, his radio having failed. All was proceeding according to plan, and the leader provided all of the usual signals to indicate that the wingman was cleared to land.

The colonel made a mistake, however, when he looked forward to continue his landing approach. Instead of sighting-in on the runway, he focused instead on the much narrower taxiway to the right of the runway. Continuing his approach, he made what I'm sure was a very passable landing. Unfortunately, he landed on the taxiway and not on the runway! Fortunately, no other aircraft were on the taxiway at that moment.

I would imagine that all seemed to go well for the colonel at first, although he may have noticed that the "runway" appeared narrower than usual. But after rolling for a few seconds, he probably looked ahead at the line of barrels and aircraft looming in the distance. It was too late to add power and take off again, so he locked his brakes and skidded to a stop, dangerously close to the barrels and lines of aircraft ahead.

Occasionally someone at the Group would put out a small and unofficial newspaper, describing the happenings at the base. The above incident prompted the preparation of a special edition. It turned out that the event had occurred on the day that the Commanding General of the First Marine Aircraft Wing was visiting the Chu Lai air base.

The description of the near-accident was a real classic, reading, "Today, Major General Louis B. Robertshaw, Commanding General, First Marine Aircraft Wing, was on hand to witness the official opening of Runway 31 Right, with Lieutenant Colonel Joe Pultorak landing his A-4 Skyhawk, coming to a smooth controlled stop, three hundred feet short of the VMA-224 barrier."

He was lucky to get it stopped!

# 26. "I CAN'T BELIEVE I'M IN VIETNAM"

JIM GRACE WAS MY MOTHER's younger brother and he had the misfortune to graduate from high school in the spring of 1942. I say misfortune because the boys that graduated that year and for the next few years had a hard experience ahead of them. This was due to America's entry into the Second World War following the Japanese attack on Pearl Harbor on December 7, 1941. They were part of America's Greatest Generation but they didn't know it yet. And many of them would never know it.

Uncle Jim joined the army and volunteered for paratrooper training. This was probably somewhat out of character for him. He was a fairly tall and slender young man who was more at ease in a musical setting. He had been an excellent high school musician and somewhat of an intellectual, perhaps a rarity among his peers in the hills of Kentucky for his time. He was ambitious and had high dreams for his future. And his future success seemed likely, considering the high regard of his friends and the respect of his teachers and adult friends within his Harlan County community of Cumberland, Kentucky.

I mention Harlan County because it was a hotbed of labor strife during that period of the late 1930's and early 1940's. The United Mine Workers of America union was struggling to unionize the coal miners and Harlan County was often in the national news. I remember seeing, as a small child, the multiple bullet holes in cars that had been used by those involved in these struggles.

A few years later my father went off to Baltimore, Maryland to work in the shipyards for a short time during the war. Once, in conversation with a fellow worker, he mentioned that he was from Harlan County in Kentucky. His co-worker took another look at Dad, saying, "I've always wanted to meet a man from Harlan County."

Another aside observation is that in James Jones's great novel, *From Here to Eternity*, the principal character was from Harlan County, Kentucky, although that fact played no part in the novel. Still, it is interesting that as Uncle Jim commenced his military training, he took a Harlan County persona along with him whether he knew it or not.

Uncle Jim was a good-looking young man and handsome in any uniform that he wore. I was four years old that summer and fall as Jim progressed in his training and I remember the photos that he sent home to his mother. My maternal grandmother lived with my step-grandfather just across the dirt road from our house on "Sanctified Hill," overlooking the eastern portion of Cumberland, Kentucky. My father's parents lived a half-mile away on a dirt road farther out along the hillside. All of the men in my family worked in the coal mines, the principal occupation available within that area.

Although Uncle Jim was to be commended for having volunteered to serve his country, his participation was cut short by a serious injury due to landing in a tree during one of his practice jumps. In the long run it may have saved his life as many of his fellow paratroopers were killed during the invasion of France in June of 1944. After convalescence, he returned to the hills of Kentucky, along with his new young bride, Ora Lee, and sat out the remainder of the war.

Uncle Jim brought one more thing back with him from the war. He had fallen into the wrong crowd and had learned the pleasures of alcoholic beverages. If consumed moderately, there is no problem. But Uncle Jim had gone beyond moderation and ultimately became an alcoholic. This affliction plagued him for the remainder of his life and probably contributed to his living a relatively short one, dying at fifty-seven years of age. It also played a great part in his inability to hold steady employment and further led to the dissolution of two marriages to two fine young women.

Uncle Jim had two sons by his first wife, Ora Lee, and two daughters by his second wife, Kathy. His first son was named James Grace, Junior and the younger son was named Donald Ray Grace. Donald was my brother's first name and Ray was my middle name, so he was named for both of us.

My family was never around any of Uncle Jim's children as they grew up, since he was off in other parts of the country while my family remained in eastern Kentucky. However, Uncle Jim had an input in my life in the summer of 1955 following my graduation from high school that spring. He had been visiting in eastern Kentucky from Michigan and was about to return there with his second family. He asked if I would like to visit with his family in Detroit and work for two months before commencing college that fall. I had no plans for the summer so quickly agreed to do so.

Being just seventeen, the best job I could get was at a supermarket. I bagged groceries, unloaded trailer trucks, and stocked shelves for fifty cents an hour that summer, the minimum wage. Two months later I arrived back home by bus with two hundred dollars to show for my efforts, and I had spent nothing during my visit. I may not have made much money, but I'm sure I gained some character, which was certainly more important at that age.

This may seem to have been a roundabout introduction, but the current story is about a day I spent in Vietnam with Uncle Jim's younger son, Donald Ray, in the summer of 1966. One day I received a letter from my mother informing me that my first cousin Donald Ray was not only in Vietnam, but apparently nearby in the Chu Lai area. She thought there might be some way I could get in touch with him. I had not seen Donald Ray since he was a small child and would not have recognized him if I had seen him. But I was certainly interested in seeing my long lost first cousin if at all possible.

I found that he was in one of the Marine infantry units guarding our Chu Lai airbase. First, I asked my commanding officer, Lt. Colonel Paul G. McMahon for permission to spend a large part of a day with him. After the visit, I would still be able to fly a late afternoon flight and a night flight as well, if required. I also asked to borrow the colonel's jeep to bring Donald Ray to the air base and later to return him to his unit. The colonel, a true gentleman with whom I later served at Headquarters, Marine Corps, graciously granted both requests.

I then called Donald Ray's commanding officer and asked if I might have him come for a one-day visit. He was agreeable and volunteered to inform Donald Ray of my plans. The day soon arrived and I drove the jeep to Donald Ray's unit. He later told me his friends were excited for him to have a lieutenant (!) as a cousin, and that he was on his way to come to visit him. They wondered how the greeting would go. Would Donald Ray salute first, and then speak? I don't remember now, but we had a warm greeting before meeting his infantry buddies.

When I arrived I found a very young and very slender young man in whom I could see my uncle's features. And just as Uncle Jim had probably been misplaced in his war, so it appeared for Donald Ray as well. He was barely eighteen, if that, as I recalled him having been born in 1948. He appeared to be too young to find himself in an infantry combat unit in Vietnam, but that is where he was.

*Donald Ray Grace near Chu Lai in 1966. Photo by the author*

We drove back to the air base and the first thing I did was to take him in to meet my commanding officer. We then toured the squadron area. We visited the flight line and watched the Skyhawks start their engines and taxi away to take off with their loads of bombs and rockets. We saw others return from their missions and watched the pilots climb down from their planes.

We took numerous pictures, including one of him sitting in my A-4 with my name on it and soon it was time for lunch. I took him with me to the officer's mess hall for what must have been a better meal than he was used to. Afterwards, I gave him a haircut.

Before my squadron had left the states, a pilot who had been in Vietnam spoke to the pilots in my squadron, telling us of what to expect upon arrival. He added, "If anyone can cut hair, be sure to take your clippers as there is no access to a civilian barbershop there." I went to the PX that very day and bought a set of clippers. I cut my own hair just days later, a practice I continued for several years, and I also cut hair for several fellow pilots while in Vietnam.

Next, we washed all of his clothes and hung them up to dry while we went for a swim at the nearby beach. When we returned to dress, I gave him new underclothes, socks and one of my shirts, which happened to be of a different design and which he was happy to acquire. We took a few more pictures including one nice one of the two of us together, him with his fresh haircut and new clothes.

*The author with his cousin Donald Ray Grace after a haircut, swim, and new clothes.*

At one point during the afternoon, as Donald Ray was living the life of Cinderella, and before he had to hurry back to his unit before the clock struck twelve, he turned to me and said, "I can't believe I'm in Vietnam." Yes, after living in tents out in the sand in the surrounding countryside, it must have seemed like another world to Donald Ray. But good things have to ultimately come to an end and I finally returned him to his unit later that afternoon.

It had been a good visit for both of us. We had made an acquaintance that had never before existed. And I was happy to give him some attention from a family that he had never known. As I drove away, I thought of his father, the uncle who had allowed me live in his home one summer eleven years earlier, enabling me to have some job experience before commencing my college years. I hadn't been able to do anything in return for my Uncle Jim, but I had enabled his number-two son to enjoy a day "out of Vietnam" at a time when I know it was much appreciated.

While leading a patrol a few months later, Donald Ray was seriously wounded by gunfire during an ambush and the ensuing firefight. The event ended his combat tour and he was returned to the states. Donald Ray has lived in Cincinnati, Ohio in the years since serving in the Marine Corps.

# 27. ASSIGNMENT TO A BATTALION

IT WAS 1966, DURING MY first year in Vietnam. I had spent the first six months at Chu Lai in VMA-311, an A-4 attack squadron. Chu Lai was a Marine air base about fifty miles down the coast from Danang, a larger air base that hosted both Marine Corps and U. S. Air Force aviation units. I felt very competent as an A-4 pilot and enjoyed the combat missions. That probably sounds odd to a civilian, for whom avoiding unnecessary danger would seem a normal and sane thing to do. But for us Marine pilots it was, "How come he has two flights tomorrow and I only have one?" or, "How come he has three flights and I only have two?" I never knew but one exception to this rule and I've written about him somewhere else.

But now I was being reassigned to serve with the ground forces of the Marine Corps there in Vietnam. Typically, the Marine Corps didn't ask for my preference. The ground side of the house needed a warm-bodied pilot to fill an Air Liaison Officer assignment and I was tagged for it (the needs of the service, etc). So I gathered my few belongings and hopped on a C-130 cargo plane for the flight up to Danang. Another flight took me further north to Dong Ha which was quite close to the DMZ. I arrived there at dusk one early November evening, beginning my five-month tour of duty with the Third Battalion of the Seventh Marine Regiment ("3/7", for short).

I met the outgoing Air Liaison Officer who was about to go out on a night patrol with a company of Marines. I probably could have gone along, but hey, even I have my limits. I didn't see the point of being initiated into the ground war in Vietnam by going on a night patrol into the DMZ on my very first night there. I was introduced to my new duties very quickly, however, and began going with a company of Marines each time they went out on an operation.

As head of the Air Liaison unit, I had a sergeant and two corporals under me. I always had two of them with me on each operation. One would carry a battery-powered UHF radio and the other carried a much lighter FM radio. The UHF radio was for communication with the jets providing close air support, if required. The FM radio was used for communication with helicopters or light, fixed-wing aircraft (Bird-dogs) who acted as spotters for the jets. It turned out that we never used the UHF radio but depended on the FM communication with the Bird-dog to relay messages.

Basically, I served the companies in three ways by coordinating all resupply, medevac, and close air support missions. Anytime we were out in the field for over a couple of days at a time, we required resupply of food and ammunition. The medevac flights are obvious in that each fire fight might end with someone wounded and sometimes worse. Less frequent were the times when close air support was provided by the jets.

The assignment of a pilot to this assignment was a wise one. There were times that the expertise of an aviator was required to bring helicopters into barely adequate and often dangerous landing zones (LZ's). This became even more critical at night, but was often necessary when some young Marine had been wounded and needed to be transported as quickly as possible back to the rear for life-saving medical care.

I wasn't in the DMZ area very long before the battalion was relocated to Dai Loc, just ten miles south of Danang. The battalion continued to send companies out on the usual operations. We walked everywhere we went when I was with the battalion at Dong Ha and Dai Loc. We always had radio contact with our base, but our only real contact was

through being supplied or sending an occasional wounded Marine back.

It was always good to get back to the base, wherever we had been. The base at Dai Loc was centered on a decades-old French fort. Our living quarters, like everywhere I was while in Vietnam, were simple and basic buildings that were called hootches. They had a floor built up off the ground and a tin roof overhead but no walls. Dai Loc was the only place where I routinely slept within mosquito nets.

We had no showers at Dai Loc so I scrounged up several angle-iron fence posts and hung them horizontally along the edge of the roof of our hootch. I located an empty 55-gallon drum and placed it at the end of the building to catch the rainwater. Although the winters were not really cold in South Vietnam, it was still quite cool on occasion. I remember my modified showers well. After removing all of my clothing, I would dip my wash-pan into the drum of water and empty it over my head and shoulders. After washing thoroughly, I would take another pan of clean water, hold it over my head and pour again, rinsing my body all at once. That was quite chilly, but I came away fully cleansed.

Cleanliness was a problem when out in the field. Sometimes we would go for days without a chance to bathe. Just finding water was often a problem. Many times we might find a well and I would shave (or sometimes even bathe) out of my helmet. We had a medical corpsman called "Doc" with us who would always check the water before we would drink it. After checking, he would tell us how many iodine pills to put per canteen of water. It might be one, two, or three. If he said to add three pills per canteen, we knew we had some really bad water. I always carried two canteens and filled them out of creeks, routinely. And I remember filling them from a rice paddy one day, even with a water buffalo standing about a hundred yards away.

On one occasion we hadn't had a bath for some time and I really wanted to be able to be clean again. Although the lines of our perimeter stopped short of a nearby creek, I went with my two radio operators for a bath. We took turns bathing while the other two stayed with the rifles, guarding our bathing moments. Looking back on it from decades later, I don't think it was a very smart thing to do. But we got away with it at the time. You don't risk your life very often just to get clean!

# 28. AN UNEXPECTED ENMITY

I WAS RECENTLY READING OF Lt. Guy Bordelon, a naval aviator who served in the U.S. Navy for twenty-seven years. He had received his flight training during the Second World War, but had seen only instructor duty before it ended. Later, during the Korean War, he was the only U.S. Navy pilot to become an ace in that conflict and he achieved this distinction while flying the F4U-5N Corsair.

This story is not about Lt Bordelon or his achievements. But within the article was the statement that he, while serving on a heavy cruiser, was unhappy at the harassment he received from his "black-shoe navy" commanding officer, who hated aviators. The navy pilots wore brown shoes with their uniforms, hence the reference to the black shoes of the regular navy establishment.

Now isn't that just a wonderful sentiment to have about other professionals, not only within the U.S. military, but within your own branch of the service as well! I recently recalled some similar experiences of my own that I had encountered during my twenty years in the Marine Corps. The experience was that of an enmity toward aviators from some officers within the ground side of the Corps.

I first observed this phenomenon while at Officer Candidate School at Quantico, Virginia in the fall of 1962. The base contains an airfield and years later I flew hundreds of hours from it in the T-28, a 1400-hp, propeller-driven aircraft. Once, during the course, a major was addressing a large number of us candidates within an auditorium. Perhaps a door or two was open. At any rate, an airplane could be heard passing overhead momentarily. Instead of just pausing until it was gone, the major said, in effect, "Every time I start talking somewhere, some damned aviator has to fly over in his airplane."

His over-reaction of frustration seemed to express something profound about his attitude toward aviators and probably Marine Corps aviation, itself. But those thoughts quickly passed as I was engrossed in trying to meet the formidable demands required in becoming an officer in the Marine Corps.

Five years later I was in my first year in Vietnam and assigned to the Third Battalion, Seventh Marines as an Air Liaison Officer. There I lived, slept, and experienced life-threatening dangers alongside the ground officers within the battalion. And, for the first time since my OCS experience, I found that the feelings the major had expressed were not uncommon among the company grade officers (captains and lieutenants) with whom I served.

One afternoon while in the field with a company, we were being resupplied with the essentials required by our men to be able to survive and fight. As the helicopter lifted off and turned back toward its base, an officer said, "Well, there he goes, back to the clean sheets, etc." I was appalled at his remark. I responded, "What do you want him to do, just park his helicopter out here in the mud and sleep with us on the ground? Who will maintain it then?"

Sometimes comments were directed at the issue of pay. Aviators (and other specialized units within the military) received incentive pay to assist in enticing highly-trained individuals to make the military a career. At the time, it probably cost a million dollars (or maybe twice that) to train a pilot to combat-level skills. It certainly made sense to offer such personnel an extra three or four thousand dollars a year rather than lose them back to the civilian world and have to train their replacements from scratch.

But sniping comments were commonplace when the subject surfaced. One cute thing I heard was, "Well, I don't begrudge him his flight pay, it's his combat pay that I resent." Okay, maybe there was supposed to be a touch of humor here. If it were not humor, it implies that aviators were not doing their part in some way. Maybe they were just flying around for the fun of it and getting to be called Marines on top of it all. It's one of those, "Smile when you say that, 'pardner'" comments. Otherwise, it comes across as a needless and malicious comment toward people who are doing the best they can at what they are trained to do.

My worst experience was one evening when we had been in the field on an operation for several days and nights. At dusk a young Marine was seriously wounded and I called for a Medevac helicopter. Within half an hour, the pilot checked in by radio as he approached our location. At about the same time I was informed that the Marine had now died of his wounds.

I informed the helicopter pilot that the WIA was now a KIA (killed in action vice wounded in action). It was a dark night by now and the landing zone was small and surrounded by a dense jungle. The pilot said, "Since our squadron is returning here tomorrow morning on a resupply mission, the KIA will be returned to base at that time." I acknowledged his message and he turned back toward his base.

A few of the ground officers who had heard the conversation spitefully said, "If that had been an air-winger down here, he would have made the effort to land and pick him up." I responded with as much patience as I could muster, saying, "Look, it is dark as hell out there tonight and there is no need to risk the loss of an aircraft and four people on board by trying to make a landing attempt into a small and dangerous LZ unless absolutely required. If the Marine were still alive, they would have made every effort to get him aboard and back to the hospital. But there is no sense in taking such a risk out there tonight." They shut up, but I am sure the feelings remained.

Why did these feelings exist? I think there were several reasons. For one thing, military pilots <u>like</u> what they do for a living, even thriving on the combat missions themselves. It's what they were trained to do and they like nothing more than strapping into a plane and going out killing as many of the enemy as they possibly can (we're talking wartime here, and enemy combatants at that). I'm sorry if that sounds offensive to anyone, but that is the aim of war---to kill them before they kill you or your people, and to get the war over with so you can get back home and live a normal life.

Maybe the ground officers are not as enthusiastic about what they do. And you have to admit, there is a John Wayne air about, quote, Marine jet pilots, unquote. And they may resent the small pay differential of a few hundred dollars a month. But I've addressed that.

I think it ultimately comes down to a form of jealousy. I think that as one trudges along at a near snail's pace and looks up at a jet roaring past overhead, there is a natural instinct to be envious, even to the point of resentment on some occasions, of the pilots flying large, powerful, fast, thunderous, and imposing aircraft, all with the apparent utmost of ease.

There have been many combat instances in the past eighty years where the survival of Marines on the ground was enhanced and even secured by the presence of Marine Corps aircraft overhead. Guadalcanal in World War II and the Chosin Reservoir in North Korea immediately leap to mind! And I know from experience that, with only one exception, every Marine Corps aviator I ever knew would have risked his life to provide close air support for the troops to the fullest extent of which his aircraft was possible.

I hope attitudes have changed within the Marine Corps in the forty-five years since the time of which I write. But human nature is resilient and once it has achieved momentum, is difficult to change. I would imagine there are still some young captains and lieutenants (and higher?) that still possess some of these needless and harmful attitudes toward the Marine Air Wings and their aviators.

# 29. A DARK AND RAINY NIGHT

"It was a dark and rainy night," as I plagiarize Snoopy of the comic strip, *Peanuts*. But first, let's set the stage.

Military pilots received flight pay when I was a pilot many years ago and I'm sure they still do. Initially, it was considered hazardous duty pay and it was there to encourage pilots to fly despite the dangers of flying. After all, some pilots are killed in service to their country each year even in peacetime. Other service members received similar incentive pay, such as paratroopers, submarine crewmembers, etc. And many of them have given their lives during peacetime as well.

To maintain qualification for flight pay, pilots were required to fly a minimum of four hours per month. Some assignments could prevent attainment of these hours so provision was made for banking of extra hours to carry over in the lean months. This situation occurred when I was assigned to a Marine battalion during my first year in Vietnam. Besides flying the hours for flight pay, however, we needed to fly regularly enough to maintain our proficiency.

I hadn't flown for six weeks when I arrived at Chu Lai by C-130 from Danang one evening. It was January of 1967 in the monsoon season and a light rain was falling under a dreary and low overcast. I checked in with the squadron I had been in for nearly six months, letting them know I would be there for a few days and that I wanted to be put on the schedule for regular combat missions. The Schedules Officer made note of it and I found a place to stay and went to bed tired that night after a long, hard day.

At about 2:00 a.m., someone woke me from a deep sleep, saying, "Captain Gibson, we have two missions for you between now and morning."

I shook myself awake, got dressed into my flight suit and boots, gathered my flight gear and walked to the Marine Air Group briefing office to be briefed for my missions. Man, it was a dark night as I trudged along!

Both missions were to be radar bombing missions, called TPQ missions after the designation of the type of radar being used. A plane would take off, contact the TPQ control facility and be directed to the target area. We would fly at an assigned altitude, airspeed and heading, normally at about 14,000 or 15,000 feet of altitude.

As we approached the position to release the bombs, we were given the call "Armstrong," which meant to turn on the master armament switch and be ready to drop the bombs. Then, moments later, we heard, "Standby, standby, Mark, Mark!" and we dropped one or two bombs as directed with a single depression of the bomb release switch. We would then repeat the cycle on different targets until all of the bombs were expended. Hopefully, we had achieved something by hitting whatever the targets were. At any rate, it would certainly rattle someone's cage for a couple of bombs to explode nearby, completely unexpectedly in the middle of the night.

I received the briefing for my missions and made my way to the flight line. There, in a light rain, I used a flashlight to help preflight the plane and bombs. It sounds odd to speak of pre-flighting bombs, but we had to check that they were properly attached to the underside of the wings with all of their necessary wires in place. Remember seeing those little propellers on the front end of bombs? When a bomb was released, a safety wire attached to the wing was pulled from the front of the bomb. This freed the propeller to commence rotation. After turning for so many revolutions during their fall, the bomb would have been armed and capable of exploding. That is one of the things we would check for on the bombs.

I finally climbed into the cockpit and strapped into the ejection seat with the aid of the plane captain. The external electrical power was then engaged. Turning on the cockpit lights, all of the red instrument panel lights illuminated. What <u>were</u> all of these gauges, anyway, after not seeing them for over six weeks? I cranked up the engine and went through the post-start checks. After calling Ground Control, I taxied through the light rain out to the runway. Switching over to the tower frequency momentarily, I was given clearance to take off and handed off to Departure Control.

Fortunately, only a light rain was falling at the time although it was as dark and foreboding as could be under the low overcast at this bleak hour of around 3:00 A.M.

I took the duty runway, as we would say, held my feet on the brakes with all my might and ran the engine to full power. A quick check of the engine gauges showed that everything was in order and I released the brakes. The plane immediately began accelerating rapidly down the dark runway. Our only runway lighting was a line of ordinary highway flare pots down each side of the runway.

The runway itself was nothing to brag about. It was a temporary field with aluminum matting laid across the runway for the full 8,000 feet of its length. Underneath the matting, the clay had settled in various places causing the runway to have a rough and slightly bouncy feel while taking off or landing. I still remember my arrival at Chu Lai by C-130 earlier in the previous year. I had never experienced a rough runway before and I remember how the C-130 bumped and jostled as it rolled to a stop on the 8,000-foot runway.

The cockpit of the A-4 was very small and in the older single-seat versions a pilot could hit each side of the canopy by merely rocking his head left or right. The runway was so rough that on this dark night my head was nearly bumping off the sides of the canopy during the takeoff roll.

The plane continued accelerating as it hurtled down the center of the runway. Finally, I saw 145 knots on the airspeed indicator and raised the nose to takeoff attitude. The plane began lifting off, and as soon as I knew I was flying, I raised the landing gear and then the flaps. The aircraft really began accelerating now and I had to lay on the nose-down trim button to keep the nose from rising. As I entered the low overcast, I was obviously flying 100% on instruments and the attitude gyro rocked back and forth in response to my rough attempts to fly after such a long layoff. Finally, I was up to climb airspeed and contacted the TPQ facility as I climbed to altitude.

The mission was uneventful and I finally returned to base for a ground-controlled radar approach down through the clouds, breaking out underneath for my landing. I parked the plane and climbed out, glad to be back on terra firma after such an experience!

After less than half an hour, I began repeating the cycle. The rain had picked up but soon I had the canopy down for the engine start and taxied out to the runway for the second time. I still remember thinking to myself as I took the duty runway, "If it had been this bad the first time, I don't think I would have gone!" But I had more confidence this time. I repeated every aspect of the previous flight and this time it wasn't nearly as harrowing of an experience.

After all, it was no longer six weeks since I had last flown!

# 30. LYING IN A RICE PADDY

It had been a hot day of traipsing through the jungles before finally stopping to rest on a long, narrow, and low ridge of built-up dirt separating some rice paddies. It was perhaps ten to twenty feet wide with lots of vegetation which prevented any cooling air flow. So I dropped down off the ridge onto the dry edge of a rice paddy and took off my helmet. Aah! That felt good to have the fresh, cool air on my head. So I slipped off my flak jacket. Aah, again! So I next took off my green shirt and then finally my green T-shirt. It was like heaven to have those hot things off and to feel the cool refreshing breeze there in the shade. Bang! Someone shot at me from rather far away as I heard the bullet land nearby. I quickly gathered up all of my things and got back up where the other Marines were, on the covered portion between the rice paddies!

We ate C-rations three times a day when in the field. I didn't mind them, myself. The rations came twelve meals per box. There was actually quite a bit of variety in the selection of meals. A retired U.S. Army friend here in DeKalb, Everett McShepard, reminded me recently that the turkey loaf meal was one of the favorites. The least favorite among the Marines was the meal containing ham and lima beans. They called them ham and mothers. I volunteered to take the meal more often than my share because I didn't mind it as badly as so many of them seemed to do.

Each meal had about a half-dozen cigarettes, which I certainly gave away. All but two of the meals included a small, single-serving packet of coffee. Those two meals had hot chocolate (!) which was considered a luxury. The only time I ever drank coffee in my life was while in the field in Vietnam. I think it was to kill the taste of the usually distasteful water that we had to settle for when in the field.

We were still at Dai Loc at Christmas of 1966. On Christmas Eve I went to a religious service. As we were leaving, the chaplain showed us a small pile of letters from school children back home and invited us to take one to answer. I probably picked up a dozen. I took them back to my hootch and wrote a nice letter back for every one that I had picked up. A couple of weeks later, I received a fat envelope in the mail. It turned out that many of the letters I had answered had come from one particular class of children somewhere in New Jersey. Enclosed was a cut-out newspaper article about some Marine captain who had spent his Christmas Eve answering letters from school-kids back home.

I probably came close to being hit many times, because I was in situations where I could sometimes hear the bullets whizzing by. But one time was especially dangerous while at Dai Loc. I had gone with a company on an extended operation that lasted practically a week. It wouldn't have taken so long, but as we were coming down off of some hills, we spotted what I took to be farmers in a field below. The company commander, however, ordered our artillery Forward Observer to call in an artillery attack upon them. There were some large boulders near our position and the first incoming shells began hitting into these boulders, much closer to us than the poor farmers leaving their fields. Corrections were quickly made and soon the farmers had left the fields.

Arriving at the bottom of the hill, I thought we would turn left and head back to Dai Loc. The company commander, however, said to me, "We're not going back in. We've just made contact!" He must have seen more militancy in those farmers in their rice paddies than I did and shortly thereafter the company began crossing one of the paddies. I was dubious but Air Liaison Officers didn't make company-level decisions. So I began crossing with the rest of the company. If the enemy had had a machine gun in the underbrush on the other side of the rice paddy, they could have wiped out every last one of us! People were getting stuck in the nearly knee-deep rice paddy and having to turn around and help those around them who were also stuck. By the grace of God, we finally made it to the other side.

An hour or so later, dusk was approaching and some of us were standing at the edge of a rice paddy in what appeared to be a graveyard. The built-up ground over the South Vietnamese graves was shaped like the cake in a strawberry short-cake. They were circular with a round indentation in the top just like the cakes.

All of a sudden, machine guns opened up and mortars began hitting nearby. I was immediately flat on my stomach in the mud behind the mound of a grave! I could see red tracers passing directly over my head and a mortar round hit in the mud not more than twenty feet behind us. The firing went on in both directions for perhaps fifteen minutes before the enemy must have had enough of it and left. After it was clear they were gone, we stood up to take stock of the situation. After learning that some men had been wounded, I called in the medevac request.

Dusk had passed and it was dark by the time the helicopter arrived. We were still on the edge of the rice paddy with trees behind us. The helo would have to land in a very shallow portion of the rice paddy between us and where the enemy had been on the other side of the paddy. I gave the pilot a recommended approach heading and told him that the friendlies would be on his right as he approached to land. I told him that any source of firing from his left side would be fair game to the gunner on that side of his aircraft.

By now it was very dark on a moonless night. Although I had indicated our position by flashlight signals, I knew he had no good reference for his landing approach. I don't like saying this because it makes me look braver than I was. But I knew that someone had to crawl out there into the paddy to show the pilot exactly where to land. I was the best qualified for the job, so you guessed it. I took an FM radio and a flashlight and crawled out into the shallow rice paddy there in the dark. I was now between the good guys and the bad guys. If the firing had commenced anew, I would have gotten to see it going by in both directions, hopefully over my head as I lay there.

To make the long story short, I talked the pilot into his touchdown point while holding a light for his reference during the approach. The wounded Marines were quickly loaded onto the CH-34 helo and he was soon gone. We had lucked out. Not a single shot was fired. But I didn't know it would be that way when I went out there. For all I knew, all hell may have broken loose again with me right in the middle of it all.

No one had told me to do what I did. And one more thing, when I returned to the safety of the remainder of the company, no ground officer ever came up and said, "Good job, Larry." It was never mentioned that I knew of and I don't mean that I should have been recommended for a medal. But it still would have been nice to have had at least some degree of appreciation. It didn't happen, though.

Sometimes our reward is something that we just have to take pride in by ourselves. I came away from the experience knowing that, when the chips were down, I had stepped forward and had risked my life for the sake of my fellow Marines. And that is better than any medal.

*The author at Dai Loc in January 1967*

105

# 31. A LETTER FROM HOME

IT WAS PROBABLY AROUND JANUARY or February of 1966. I don't remember anything about the day except that I was out on some kind of operation with one of the companies of Marines. We had stopped for the day and were settling down to spend the night out in the field, as they liked to say in the Marine Corps.

It was a fairly hilly region and a bomb had hit on a hillside, clearing out a nice, ready-made foxhole. It may have been oversized, but I decided to use it as my home on this dark and drizzly night. I attached my shelter-half (half of a pup-tent, normally attached to the half provided by another Marine to form a shared tent) to the uphill side of my newly-designated foxhole and propped it up in some fashion on the lower side. It was large enough that when I got inside, it was quite roomy with a little bit of vertical space as well. When darkness arrived, I would be prepared and ready for bed in a reasonably dry and comfortable spot.

An H-34 helicopter arrived with supplies at dusk and I thanked the pilot over the radio as he headed back towards Danang, some twenty miles away. My two radio operators then joined with me for a supper of C-rations.

I always thought C-rations got pretty bad press. But then again, I didn't eat them for days and days on end like so many of the ground combat personnel had to do when nothing else was available. I will therefore defer to those who did so to provide the definitive evaluation of their suitability. I found them to be very satisfactory for my use, but I am pretty easy to please, having only a very short list of things I don't prefer to eat: asparagus, beets and mushrooms. Since those were not in the C-ration menus, I was okay. (See C-Rations at the appendix for a summary of the contents of the individual rations).

The C-rations came in a sturdy, flat, cardboard case of twelve individually-packed meals. Some of the meals were favorites and some were avoided whenever possible. However, dispensing of the meals was generally accomplished in a fair manner, with people taking turns at the former and the latter.

All of the meals were contained in the usual steel cans, just like our cans of vegetables back home, except they were all of the Marine Corps green color. Without one important small item, however, we would have really had a problem. That item was a can-opener. Fortunately, that problem had been solved way back in 1942 during World War II, when a very small hand-operated opener had been developed. It has often been referred to as the Army's greatest invention.

The openers had a small hole drilled in one end that enabled them to be carried on the dog-tag chains we wore around our necks. You can find them on the internet by searching for can opener, P-38. They were nicknamed P-38's because it supposedly required that number of operations to open a C-ration can. I never heard them called that. If I had, I'm sure I would have counted to check the accuracy of the nickname.

Everyone had a few of these small can-openers, and maybe half a dozen of them were in each case of C-rations in case we ever lost one. They were flat when not in use, with a sharp little curved blade that could be turned up by about ninety degrees on one side. Although only an inch and a half or so long, they were ingeniously designed and could be used to cut the top off a can of food nearly as well as standard, hand-held can-openers back in the states.

Now that the food and the openers have been described, there was only one more requirement for enhancement of our meals---that was heat. You would be surprised to know that we (nearly) always had hot food when out in the field. Granted, it wasn't heated and served to us, nor did we sit at some comfortable table. Instead, we used heat tabs to heat our meals individually. These tabs were little bluish objects about the size of a fifty-cent coin and perhaps a quarter of an inch thick. When ignited, they burned with a bluish flame, as I recall. They gave off quite a bit of heat that would last long enough to heat our meal's major entrée and a cup of coffee.

Everyone would have saved one of the small cans from a previous meal, usually one of about two inches in height. Using our can-opener, we would cut holes around the bottom and top of the cans for ventilation to enhance the burning of the tab. Having opened our can of beans, or whatever, the heat tab would be placed in the ventilated can and ignited. Placing the larger can on top of the stove would result in warm food within just a few minutes. The stove can would be retained and used until finally no longer usable.

One variation was the heating of liquids in our metal canteen cups, as I recall. Another variation involved the use of a small foldable grill that was perhaps four or five inches square on top, with two sides that folded out from underneath to support it. These may have been sent from home or purchased at a PX at some time. I don't remember. Some people might not think the C-ration meals were very good but I always enjoyed mine, whatever the particular meal may have been.

There wasn't much to do so we would turn in for the night pretty quickly. Later, I was in my fox-hole, reading something by flashlight, when someone outside my shelter called my name. I raised the flap of my shelter-half and was handed a letter. In addition to the supplies, the helicopter had brought out the latest mail and it was finally being delivered around through the company.

I leaned back against the bank there with a light rain falling on my tent and opened my mail. I don't remember now if it was from my wife or my parents. But I still remember the feeling of warm security there under my shelter as I read by flashlight of the news from home. I was in my own little world that evening. Granted, it may have been in Vietnam, and there was an enemy out there that would have loved to kill me. But it seemed far removed at the moment as I relaxed before folding the letter, turning off my flashlight, and going off to well-deserved sleep with all of my clothes and boots on. I had finished another day in Vietnam.

The letters from home told us there were loved ones in the world that cared about of us and missed us and looked forward to our return. The letters were from a rational world, one where people didn't carry weapons or worry about stepping on a booby trap or the like. And it was a world of colors beyond the green of the trees, brown of the soil, and the blue of the sky that we saw each day.

I remember when I was at OCS at Quantico. The only colors we saw inside the buildings all week were gray and green. When we were given time off on Saturday afternoons, I would sometimes walk to the base PX and marvel at all of the brilliant and different colors. Today, when I go to the PX or commissary, fifty years later, the same multitude of colors present a strain to these older eyes, and I am much more comfortable when I can finally leave the building.

It was interesting to me when in Vietnam that I was on the opposite side of the world from my family back home. I would sometimes think of their day beginning as darkness came over my portion of the world. When I was in Japan in 1977, one of my friends once told me of his plane having been hit by enemy fire in Vietnam at a certain time one afternoon. In a letter from his wife a few days later, she told of how she had awakened abruptly at that exact time in the middle of the night back home. She had a sense of foreboding and associated it with her husband's danger in Vietnam. I'm just relating what my friend related to me, in all seriousness. I'm sorry that I don't recall his name.

I even once wrote a song about the phenomenon of our opposite nights and days. It also occurred during my third overseas tour, while at MCAS Iwakuni in Japan. The name of the song was, "Tonight I'm on the Wrong Side of the World".

Life wasn't easy for the families back home, either. During my first year in Vietnam, my daughter Carolyn was an infant when I left home and nearly two years old upon return. During the second year in Vietnam, my wife June had two small children to care for, what with my son Arlan having been born between the trips overseas.

The war in Vietnam was ubiquitous in the news on television and in the newspapers of the time. I remember seeing the news programs when back in the states. Sometimes I might even see an A-4 making some kind of attack. It would have been very stressful for a wife or the parents of our nation's fighting men, just as it had been in all wars before and has been in all of the wars since. My wife later told me of how she feared having a black government car pull up in front of the house bringing terrible news.

It can be said that, "They also served." It wasn't just the service members in the combat area. It affected the wives and families and parents and all others who cared. The sacrifices of the service members were mirrored by those of the loved ones that stayed behind. Our nation owes them a debt of gratitude as well.

*The author going flying at Chu Lai, 1966*

*VMA-311 A-4E going to war at Chu Lai in 1966. Photo by the author.*

*The author with Darrell Smith at Iwakuni, Japan, 1966*

*Darrell Smith in VMA-211 A-4C over Iwakuni, Japan in 1966. Photo by the author.*

*Lieutenants Lou Shikany, George "Top" Felt, the author, and
Leo Holler after receiving their first air medals.*

*The author sitting on a VMA-311 bomb cart*

*The author returning from an outdoor shower at Chu Lai in 1966*

*Marine Corps CH-46 helicopter, 1966. Photo by the author.*

*A VMA-211 A-4E over MCAS Iwakuni, Japan. Photo by the author*

*The author and Major Don Gascoigne, XO of VMA-311, Chu Lai, 1966*

*A-4C Skyhawk ready for a mission at Chu Lai. Photo by the author*

*C-130 landing at Chu Lai. Photo by the author*

# 32. MIDNIGHT MEDEVAC

It goes without saying that many military personnel die of wounds sustained in combat. Just think of how horrific it must have been in battles over the centuries when there was no appreciable medical care at all. By World War II, modern medical techniques, improved medicines and blood and plasma transfusions enabled many of the wounded to survive that would certainly have died in previous wars. The concept of Mobile Army Surgical Hospitals (MASH units) was also introduced in the latter years of that war.

The Korean War in the early 1950's brought further improvements with the use of light aircraft and especially the use of helicopters to move the wounded from the battlefield to medical care within a minimum amount of time. Also, as we have seen in the TV series MASH, the abilities of such surgical hospitals was further advanced by then. These improvements enabled tens of thousands of our wounded personnel to survive that would otherwise have been lost.

By the time of the Vietnam War, all of these practices had been improved to near their present state. The capability of helicopters had also continued to improve, enabling the wounded personnel to receive medical care while being transported to medical facilities at reasonably high rates of speed. The CH-34 helicopter (built by Sikorsky) was the primary medevac aircraft I observed during my assignment to the ground Marines in 1966 and 1967. It was powered by a radial, reciprocating engine, vice the gas turbine (jet) engines of the UH-1 Huey and other helicopters of the period.

The CH-34 was a general-purpose helicopter that provided all of our routine resupply and medevac needs. For larger-scale troop movement or sustained movement of material, the heavier CH-46 was used. And, starting in 1967 I believe, the even larger CH-53 came into use. It was valued so highly that I recall the joke that the Viet Cong and North Vietnamese soldiers were forbidden to fire at it.

In an earlier story, I told of being on the hot pad at Chu Lai, ready to respond in the A-4 Skyhawk to any emergency close-air-support mission that might arise. Later, I will speak of being on call in the twin-engine, propeller-driven R4D, ready to launch and provide illumination for ground troops under attack during the night. I was never around helicopter bases, but obviously they had crews and aircraft on standby both night and day to respond to requests for emergency medevac missions.

Such missions would have required highly-experienced aircrew personnel. There was no way to foresee what conditions they might be launched into on any given day or night. The night missions would certainly have been even more hazardous, because we humans just don't see very well in the dark! And the helicopters would have had to descend and land into very inhospitable and dangerous landing sites (called landing zones, or LZ's for short). All of that, plus the possibility that someone might be shooting at you all of the time as well! My hat is off to the helicopter pilots. We jet pilots would fly over the targets at over 500 mph and think we were doing something. The helo pilots would slow down to a hover! That was pure guts all of the way!

I told an earlier medevac story that I named "Lying in a Rice Paddy." The current story likewise occurred at night but at least I was on dry land. It occurred around March of 1967 when "3/7" (Third Battalion, Seventh Marines) was down in the Duc Pho area. I was with a company out in the field on an operation of some sort for a few days and nights. I don't remember details of the operation. All I remember is the medevac mission that occurred one night around midnight.

It was a dark night and we had bedded down for the night out in the boonies. Fortunately, we were adjacent to a fairly large opening in the area that was otherwise covered by trees and the jungle. As you might imagine, there was no entertainment out there. This was in the time before cell phones, the internet or other electronic paraphernalia. All you could do was heat up your C-rations for supper, sit around for a while and then go to bed there on the ground.

Sometime around midnight, I was awakened and informed that a Marine had been wounded. An enemy soldier of some sort (Viet Cong, etc) had slipped closer and closer to one of our outposts. He had thrown a grenade into one of the foxholes and a Marine had been wounded and needed medical evacuation. I called the appropriate agency and provided the information they needed, including our location and the number of wounded personnel. After that, the Marine was given treatment by our assigned corpsman while the helicopter made its way to us.

Soon, the helicopter checked in on our radio frequency, providing an estimate of how much longer it would take to arrive at our location. Finally, I could see his lights approaching in the sky to the north. In my first call to him, I identified myself as Crepe Myrtle One Four, Actual. Crepe Myrtle was our battalion call sign. Crepe Myrtle One was the commanding officer's call sign. Crepe Myrtle Two was the executive officer's call sign, etc. Crepe Myrtle One_Four was pretty far down the list, being the call sign of the Air Liaison Officer.

One other practice is that anyone on the air liaison team could use the Crepe Myrtle One Four number just as the commanding officer's radio operator could use Crepe Myrtle One. But when the radio transmission included the word Actual, it signified that the top man himself was making the call. When making my initial contact with a helicopter pilot, I always used Crepe Myrtle One Four Actual in the transmission so the pilot would know that he was talking to another pilot just like himself. That meant a lot to the helo pilot and gave him a higher degree of confidence in the contents of the ensuing communications.

I radioed him that I was down at his 11:00 o'clock position with a flashlight and he reported that he had visual contact. I then informed him that we had a very adequate LZ but there was a pretty good wind coming out of the west-northwest at maybe 10 knots or so. In my radio call, I was even more specific and estimated the wind to be out of about 290 degrees. He then turned off his lights and commenced his descent. I could not see him thereafter until I heard his engine and saw his outline as he approached the LZ.

Big mistake! He was coming in from exactly the wrong direction! Airplanes and helicopters take off and land <u>into</u> the wind, not with it at their backs. I could see him trying to slow the helo down as his nose rose to counter the effect of the wind carrying him toward the trees. After nearly stopping the movement over the ground, he then commenced a turn, but not a turn like we do in a car. Instead, the helo was at a near hover, but still being carried slowly toward the trees at the end of the LZ while he was rotating the helo around to face the wind. I could see what he was doing and just kept my mouth shut to keep from distracting him.

He finally got the helo turned around into the wind and after that it was relatively easy for him to make his landing. The wounded Marine was loaded aboard and within minutes the helo had lifted off for its return trip back to the base.

After seeing him get safely airborne and realizing that he could now accept a radio call, I asked, "Didn't you hear me say that the wind was out of 290?" He responded, uncritically, "Yes, we screwed it up."

Once again we see that we can all make mistakes. Someway he had misconstrued my message about the wind direction and thought he had to make his approach from that direction. He could have easily been blown into the trees during the landing attempt and then we would have <u>really</u> needed a medevac aircraft! We would have had a downed, crashed helicopter with all four crewmembers either killed or severely wounded. Like I said before, it takes guts and tremendous ability to do what they had to do, even in their routine medevac missions.

We were all lucky on that dark midnight occasion, and I give thanks for the bravery and dedication of our fantastic Marine Corps helicopter pilots!

# 33. "GOING BY THE BOOK"

THE A-4 SKYHAWK, LIKE PROBABLY most combat planes, had a trigger on the control stick right where your trigger finger touches the stick. The bomb release "pickle button" was also on the stick, right where your thumb would naturally apply it. It was obviously important to keep your finger and thumb off these two switches unless it was desired that something be fired or dropped. But there was an overriding switch that prevented these two switches from actuating the guns or bombs, even if they were unintentionally depressed. That was the master armament switch.

Back in the states, we pilots did things by the book by waiting until we had rolled in on our attack run and had the gunsight on the target before turning on the master armament switch. The procedure existed for safety reasons. If the master armament switch was in the ON position, the pilot could inadvertently fire the guns or drop a bomb if the guns or bomb release switches were accidentally depressed. We had followed this procedure through hundreds of practice attack runs of gunnery and bombing practice.

Upon arrival in Vietnam, however, we were told to discontinue this procedure. Instead, once we were in the target area and ready to commence attacking runs, we were to turn the master armament switch on and leave it on until our runs were completed. True, the possibility of inadvertently firing or dropping something still existed. But in the first place, whatever was fired or dropped would be hitting someplace in Vietnam, which would normally be no big thing.

Secondly, it was better to leave the switch on than to forget to turn the switch on during an attack and end up making a "dry" attack run for nothing. And finally, once the pilot rolled in with his gunsight on the target, the last thing he wanted to do was put his eyes back into the cockpit to reach for the master switch, and then look back out to re-acquire the target.

This became our standard procedure very quickly and we learned to fly as we had never flown before. Now we flew with our trigger finger and right thumb always clear of their respective switches. It was so important that it became a part of our habit pattern and I flew that way all the time, whether on a combat mission or not. I remember coming back home to the States and continuing to fly that way for quite some time before the habit pattern finally went away.

Some pilots may have refused to change, however. After all, doing things by the book had been preached to us ever since we had commenced flying. And one pilot that did not change came within a hair of killing me. And he <u>did</u> hit the Marine lying beside me one afternoon in February of 1967.

Our battalion had recently been airlifted by CH-46 helicopters into the Duc Pho area, farther south than in previous locations. It was a dangerous area as U.S. forces had not operated there before and we were attacked by machine guns and mortars the very first night we were there. Fortunately, I was able to clamber out of my two-man pup tent and leap into the foxhole I had dug before dark. Later, I assisted in completing the medevac requirements for those Marines who had been wounded in the attack. The next morning, I was told to go get a weapon as I would be going with a company of Marines on an operation.

I walked over to what was considered our armory and saw some weapons laid out on the ground. The sergeant asked me, "Do you want a Thompson 'Tommy gun,' a 'grease gun,' an M-14 rifle, or this twelve-gauge shotgun?" Without hesitation, I said I would take the shotgun. After all, I was with fifty or sixty Marines and they all had rifles or machine guns. I figured that if the enemy ever broke through all of that, I would prefer to have the shotgun as my last line of defense. He then said, "I hope it serves you better than the last guy that carried it."

Over the next few months, numerous firefights took place and I took the shotgun off of safety several times but I never fired it. I had told myself I would not just fire into the bushes, but would fire only if I absolutely knew that it was the enemy that I could see. But that never happened.

*The author near Duc Pho in March 1967*

We often had air support by helicopters and occasionally by jets. Sometimes the bombs would hit so close to our position that some of the pieces of shrapnel would literally fall down around us. And, boy! The bombs were really loud when hitting that close.

One afternoon we were in the northern end of a village with a rice paddy between us and the enemy. They were in another village just to the north of us. Two A-4's were conducting an airstrike for us. They had been dropping 250-pound Snake-eye bombs but were now down to just their 20-millimeter cannons. I was lying on the side of a bank beside the company commander, a tall captain of about 6'2". I was communicating by FM radio with a light plane (Bird-dog) overhead, who in turn communicated with the jets by UHF radio.

The company commander told me to request that the jets make their final runs in the northern part of the village opposite us. Before the next run occurred, I still remember easing myself further up the bank, lying on my left side with my legs tucked up under my butt. I did this because I am only 5'7" or so and could not adequately observe the attack. I will never forget looking back down at the company commander's legs. He was tall and didn't have to move further up the bank like I did.

The next thing I knew, I felt as though we had been bombed! I could not see the planes in their runs because of the trees around us and the pilot had mistakenly strafed the northern portion of the wrong village, namely, our position! A 20-millimeter round had passed directly under my butt, missing me literally by inches, and had struck the company commander, taking off his left leg just below the knee. If I had not moved less than ten seconds prior, the round would have hit me at about waist level, killing me instantly.

The pilot had stitched a line of 20-millimeter rounds up through the length of the entire company. Miraculously, only one man had been hit---the company commander! I immediately called off the airstrike, told the bird-dog pilot overhead to send a medevac helicopter ASAP, and applied a tourniquet to the captain's leg above the knee.

Weeks later I had occasion to talk with the pilot that had made this horrendous error, one that we pilots dreaded more than any other. He was a fine and experienced aviator. It turned out that he was going by the book in his attacks. After rolling in on the target each time, he would reach down and turn on the master armament switch. This time, however, when he looked back up and through the windscreen, his gunsight was centered on the wrong village.

The error was made on this occasion because he was, "going by the book."

# 34. HOSPITAL PATIENT
# OVER NORTH VIETNAM

U.S. MILITARY PILOTS HAVE A complete physical exam once a year, around the time of their birthday. It is called a flight physical and normally is no big thing. The pilots are generally young and in good physical condition and if there is a problem with enlargement of anything, it's just their egos. Hey! How can you blame them? As a Marine Corps recruiting slogan went back in the 1970's, "When you're the greatest, it's hard to be humble!" Okay, maybe I'm exaggerating a little, but the point is that the pilots aren't expecting any bad news from the physical and there generally is none.

In 1976 a Russian fighter pilot, Victor Belenko, defected to the west in his Mig-25 fighter, a plane that was regarded by the west as the highest performance fighter plane in the Russian Air Force inventory at the time. Victor took off from Siberia and landed at an airport in Japan, barely making it there without running out of fuel. He later wrote a book named *Mig Pilot*, about his experiences as a Russian fighter pilot and how he achieved his freedom by defecting to the west. It is a worthwhile book for anyone to read because he tells what life was like in the Soviet Union during the years leading up to 1976.

Victor told an amazing story and it turned out that the Mig-25 had been much overrated by the military forces of the western world. But, as a pilot, the thing that stood out to me was that Victor wrote that the pilots were physically examined by a doctor on every day that they flew. Perhaps it wasn't quite as thorough as our annual physical, but it was a flight physical, nonetheless.

In 1980, I was honored to hear him speak to all of the pilots at our base. One of the things he said was, "If you want to know what life is like in the Soviet Union, read the book, *Animal Farm*, by George Orwell." I went out and bought it right away. If you haven't read it, do so. It is a classic and really worth reading.

I was in my first year in Vietnam in 1966 when the time arrived for my annual flight physical. I had been assigned to the Third Battalion, Seventh Marine Regiment for a couple of months but had occasionally made my way back to the airbase at Chu Lai to fly combat missions in the A-4 Skyhawk. There were several reasons for this. In the first place, I was a pilot and was expected to maintain my flight proficiency. Secondly, pilots were required to fly a minimum of four hours per month to qualify for their flight pay. And finally, all of us normal, red-blooded American jet pilots wanted to fly the combat missions. If you didn't want to fly the missions, you were in the wrong business.

My trip to Chu Lai at this time was therefore for two reasons. One was to fly as many missions as I could accomplish in the few days available. The other was to get my annual physical done. I scheduled the physical exam and reported at the assigned time.

And, there was a problem! The chest x-ray revealed a spot on my left lung and I was temporarily grounded until further notice. This was serious! The flight surgeon said I might never fly again! I remember leaving the infirmary where the physical exam had been conducted. I heard the jets overhead, returning from their missions. And I looked off into the distance, watching an A-4 making its landing. It brought momentary tears to my eyes to think I might never get to fly military planes again.

I was sent to the larger base at Danang, Vietnam, about 50 miles north of Chu Lai, where I was admitted to the base hospital. The ignominy of it all! To think that I, a big, rough, and tough Marine, that only a few days before was carrying a gun through the jungles of Vietnam, was now reduced to wearing a blue gown and flip-flops and sleeping on a hospital bed! By the way, I was only big and tough in my own mind, being about five feet, seven inches tall and weighing around 140 pounds after eight months in Vietnam.

Once the medical people get hold of you, you don't belong to yourself any more. Days pass with nothing being done. You lose your keen fighting edge (that is, if you ever had one) and you begin to grow softer. After several days, I was transported by helicopter out to the USS Repose, a U.S. Navy hospital ship serving off Danang during the Vietnamese War. There, more x-rays were taken and it was finally determined that it was not as serious as the flight surgeon had initially thought, and I was returned to the hospital at Danang.

*Marine Corps CH-34 helicopter leaving USS Repose near Danang in March 1967. Photo by the author*

They insisted that I remain attached to the hospital as a patient for a little longer, pending further paperwork. But since I was obviously an ambulatory patient, I requested permission to go back to Chu Lai for a visit of a few days. Fortunately, the request was granted. When I arrived at Chu Lai, I immediately went to see the flight surgeon and recounted what had taken place. After hearing of what had transpired, he responded to my pleas by granting me a return to an up flying status. Hurray! I could fly again!

I reported to the A-4 squadron I had been flying with, informing them that I was ready to resume flying. The next day, I was returned to the flight schedule. My first flight was into North Vietnam with two other A-4's, performing dive-bombing attacks on targets there, whatever they were, forty-five years ago.

I'll never forget the feeling as we returned southward, out over the water on our way back to Chu Lai. Flying along at 300 knots with my two friends in their A-4's, the thought came to me, "What if I had been shot down and captured on this mission? How could it have ever been explained that a bonafide patient in the Danang Naval Hospital had just been shot down over North Vietnam on a combat mission?"

# 35. HO CHI MINH WAS A FOOL

A VERY BRIEF HISTORY LESSON---A group of nations collectively termed Indochina (consisting basically of Vietnam, Cambodia and Laos) was administered as a colony by France, beginning in the late 1800's. This colony of Indochina was lost to Japan following an invasion at or near the outbreak of World War II.

Nearly four years later, after the allied victory over Japan in 1945, France attempted to reinstate their dominion over what had been their colony prior to the war. Communist forces under the leadership of Ho Chi Minh had fought against the Japanese during the war and continued their efforts against the French in the following years. These efforts climaxed in 1954 when the communist forces defeated France in a final, decisive battle at Dien Bien Phu, located west of Hanoi in the northern half of present day Vietnam.

Following this defeat for France, the Geneva Conference produced what were named the Geneva Accords in 1954. These accords separated Vietnam into two zones, the north under communist rule (the Democratic Republic of Vietnam) and the southern zone (The State of Vietnam), later called South Vietnam. Elections were to be held in 1956 with the purpose of unifying the country into one entity. However, officials from the south recognized that free elections would not be possible under the harsh communist rule in the north and the election was never conducted.

Guerilla warfare was continued by North Vietnam against the south in the years after 1954 while the U.S. attempted to stabilize the government of South Vietnam through assistance programs and eventually by providing military advisors to help stave off the guerillas. This was a time of communist ascendancy and expansion, and America was concerned with what was called the Domino Theory.

The Domino Theory, in simple terms, was that the communists would continue to gain one small country after another until they had finally conquered all of Southeast Asia. Vladmir Lenin had stated this same long term goal for conquering the entire world by communism, back in the 1920's. Although Ho Chi Minh obviously did not personally manage the entire North Vietnamese war effort, he was their national leader during this entire era and symbolized their goals and basic strategies until his death in 1969 at the age of 79.

I arrived in South Vietnam in early March of 1966 and immediately began flying combat missions in the A-4 Skyhawk from the Marine Corps air base at Chu Lai. Our missions consisted of close air support for the Marine ground forces, strategic bombing missions in Laos over the Ho Chi Minh Trail, helicopter escort missions and miscellaneous strategic attacks against Viet Cong and North Vietnamese strongholds or the locations of their provisions. These latter missions, as well as the close air support missions, were conducted under the direction of light aircraft called Bird-dogs.

Guerilla warfare is totally unlike what America faced against the Japanese and German forces during World War II. There were no front lines and I never saw an enemy soldier, while on the ground or from the air. Unless in an attack run, we remained high above the fray, so to speak. There was no need to be lower until executing the various attack runs. We then pulled out at 450 knots (about 500 mph), clearing the ground by 1,500 feet in normal dive bombing runs. In strafing runs or when dropping napalm or snake-eyes, we pulled out at about one hundred feet over the treetops. So we didn't see a lot of detail in either case, particularly considering we were usually over jungle terrain.

Even over the Ho Chi Minh Trail in Laos, it was rare to actually see the enemy trucks. They were smart enough to travel at night and park under the trees during the daytime. Here also, our forces used light aircraft, with the call-sign of Hound-dog, just as the call-sign of Bird-dog was used in South Vietnam. The pilots would fly relatively low and slow, compared to the jets. With these speed and altitude advantages for purposes of observation, they could sometimes locate the enemy in the jungles along the roads.

When the jets arrived overhead, the target would be marked by a smoke rocket and the bombing would commence. Once the first bomb was dropped, succeeding attacks were always directed by the Hound Dog in reference to the previous hit, such as "30 meters at five o'clock," etc.

The attack squadrons would have scheduled times for their flights to appear overhead and contact the individual Hound-Dogs on assigned UHF frequencies. He would describe the targets, provide target elevation, recommend attack headings, and provide any other helpful information to assist us in making an effective attack.

During my first tour in 1966, we would take our attacks to tree-top level. And it was certainly exciting on those isolated times when we actually saw the enemy trucks. One of my favorite memories in all of my missions was once when I was in the number four position of a four-plane attack mission. We had bombed and strafed perhaps half of a dozen trucks and in my final run, I strafed what appeared to be the last of the trucks. I strafed with my 20-mm cannons, pulling out at 450 knots at about 100 feet over the truck. As I pulled up, I banked the plane into a left climbing turn and looked back over my left shoulder, just in time to see the truck explode after absorbing the 20-mm hits. I hasten to add that in 1969, when I returned for my second combat tour, we were told to never go lower than 3,000 feet above the ground. Apparently their anti-aircraft capabilities had improved during my absence.

Seeing the truck explode was an isolated experience. It was far more common to return from a mission after having seemingly bombed nothing but trees. That is an unfair assessment of the effectiveness we were probably actually having. Still, when you're flying missions, you would like to have a little more positive feedback on what you are trying to accomplish. For that reason, the close air support missions were the preferred ones.

Sometimes the word might be relayed back to our base that a certain flight had been particularly effective, perhaps even stating the number of "KBA's" (killed by air) that we had achieved. Butch Miller and I were once told of having a fairly large number of KBA's after a close air support mission. And that was on a separate mission from another one that he and

I had flown together and that I have previously written about. It doesn't sound very nice in peacetime, but the objective was to kill as many of them as possible before they killed our men. That way, we could win the war and go home---and help to defeat communism at the same time!

Still, it often seemed to us that we were not achieving as much against the enemy as we would have liked. To be fair, we were getting a very narrow view of the war so all we could do was to do our best and hope that all combined efforts were proceeding toward ultimate success.

I remember sitting on the edge of a cot talking to another young pilot in the summer of 1966. We were both First Lieutenants. I remember so clearly saying, "I don't mind fighting for my country and even dying for it if need be. But I don't want to lose my life in this war, because, mark my words, in less than ten years we will be out of here and everything we are building will be being used by the communists and every dollar and life will have been spent in vain." For the record, America was gone for good in 1975, one year ahead of my prediction. Even suspecting that this would be the end result, I still flew my missions to the best of my ability.

I recall a second conversation a little later, this time with the Executive Officer of my squadron. I suggested that the overall American military effort would have been more effective if we would blockade the main seaports of North Vietnam, namely Hanoi and Haiphong. This, coupled with an unlimited bombing effort against the military targets in North Vietnam, might convince them to end their guerilla warfare against South Vietnam. He quickly assured me that this would be reckless on our part and could possibly bring China into the war.

In the spring of 1967, my first tour in Vietnam was drawing to a close. I remember a third similar conversation, with yet another pilot. By now, the war in Vietnam was extremely unpopular back home, even though our overall effort appeared to be bearing fruit. I had finally realized that Ho Chi Minh was failing to see how he could win his war in the most economical and effective manner. I maintained that all he had to do to win was to pull some of his units back into North Vietnam, tell the others to draw back into the jungles, and avoid contact with the American forces.

I could see what would have happened. America would have interpreted this as a victory for our forces and we would have left South Vietnam in a minimum number of months. We would have declared victory and gone home! Ho Chi Minh could have then re-committed his forces and renewed his attacks against the South Vietnamese forces. Do you think American public opinion would have ever allowed American forces to return to Vietnam? No way! In reality, Ho Chi Minh was almost certainly not making these strategic decisions. His name is used only to make the point and because he represented the North Vietnamese leadership.

Finally, in the fall of 1972, President Nixon ordered that American air and naval power be finally used as I had suggested six years earlier. The U.S. Navy mined the North Vietnamese harbors, ending North Vietnam's capability to be resupplied. Simultaneously, the USAF B-52's made effective and punishing raids on the enemy, in both South and North Vietnam. The ultimate effect of these combined efforts was to bring the North Vietnamese to the negotiating table and a peace treaty was signed.

Shortly thereafter, the American forces continued their departure from South Vietnam and turned the war over to the South Vietnamese. North Vietnam then did what I had earlier said they should do in order to win the war. In violation of the great and much heralded peace treaty, they brought their forces again to bear against the South Vietnamese. Within a few months it was all over. They had won the war.

I read of an interesting conversation between an American general and a North Vietnamese diplomat that took place a few years after the war. The general stated, "We never lost a single battle." The Vietnamese diplomat responded, "That is irrelevant." They had won the war in U. S. public opinion, and that was all it took.

I certainly was no military theorist or expert. But it is interesting that a mere first lieutenant could predict how the north could win the war while sitting on the edge of a cot on a hot summer day over six years ahead of its actual happening. And Ho Chi Minh, the celebrated guerilla expert, could not see the same steps to his desired victory.

To have not seen this obvious method of winning his war in the quickest and most effective manner, and to have needlessly caused the loss and maiming of so many of his people, and to have had so much infrastructure needlessly destroyed, I concluded that, "Ho Chi Minh was a fool!"

# 36. TAILWHEELER CHECKOUT

THE LANDING GEAR ON AIRCRAFT is universally one of two kinds. It is either of a tricycle design or of one utilizing a tailwheel. Within a few years after the Wright brothers first flew, the design of landing gear had stabilized into the standard tailwheel design that would remain essentially the same for the next 35 years. There were a few exceptions, but for the most part, every aircraft had a wheel under each wing (or at least one on each side, somewhere up front) and a smaller tailwheel at the rear.

Then, by the late 1940's, the tricycle design had become more common and by the end of the decade, all new aircraft were of that design, except for some small civilian planes. The advantages of the tricycle design are obvious. During ground operations, the pilot has a much better field of view, and, even more importantly, the aircraft is easier to land. This is because the center of gravity of the plane is ahead of the main landing gear resulting in higher stability during the landing roll. The center of gravity for tailwheel-type airplanes is behind the main landing gear, and is therefore much less stable, particularly during cross-wind landings.

Today almost all pilots learn to fly in airplanes having tricycle-type landing gear. And after having learned in these planes, they are generally not able to just get into a "tail-wheeler," as they are called, and be able to land it successfully. Since there are relatively few planes around of that design, it doesn't present a problem. And those pilots who do fly tail-wheelers are looked upon with a little more awe and respect by the remainder of the flying community.

Let me give you a surprising example. While a student at the U. S. Naval Test Pilot School at Patuxent River, Maryland, I once flew with a highly experienced navy test pilot in the 1946 Taylorcraft I owned at the time. I demonstrated several landings and then had him try to emulate the high degree of precision with which I made all of my landings (Ahem!).

Unfortunately, after touching down, he was slow to perceive the drifting of the tail of the plane and I had to take control of the aircraft each time to prevent the possibility of what is called a ground loop. I hated to do it, because this man was a far greater aviator than I would ever be. But he couldn't land the tailwheel plane successfully! Or at least I was unwilling to risk my much-loved airplane in the hopes that he would eventually get it right! This pilot went on to become one of the commanders of the Space Shuttle! Fortunately, the Shuttle had tricycle-type landing gear!

I commenced flight training in 1963 and had never flown a tailwheel airplane before 1967. That is when I received my tailwheel checkout at a small civilian airfield by the name of Downer Airport, located a few miles northeast of Meridian, MS. Mr. Charles E. Downer, Jr., who owned it for decades, once told me that he had bought the entire airfield in a process of sealed bids.

He said that Lauderdale County had commenced building this field as a county airport because ground fog problems were interfering with Delta Airline operations at Key Field, the major airport in Meridian. Construction had commenced prior to World War Two but had been stopped upon the outbreak of the war. After World War Two, the Lauderdale County board of supervisors declared its unfinished airport to be surplus property and sold it as Mr. Downer had described.

The airfield probably enjoyed its greatest heyday as a civilian airport in the late 1960's, which happened to be the years when I was flying there. Upon return from Vietnam in the spring of 1967, I was assigned as a flight instructor at NAS Meridian. My father-in-law, Hubert McKee, had begun taking lessons at Downer Airport while I was overseas. His instructor was a grizzled old army pilot named R. L. Tinsley. Mr. Tinsley had probably flown nearly every operational plane that the U.S. Army Air Corps had in its inventory during World War Two. I refer to him as old, although he probably wasn't over fifty years of age. But when you're just twenty-nine years old, a combat veteran of his WWII experience takes on more apparent age and authority than mere years could describe.

Hubert told me of his first instructional flight, which happened to be in a 1946 Aeronca Champ, a famous tailwheeler of the years following the war. Mr. Tinsley's instructional technique was to just let Hubert try to take off all on his own, probably with very little warning of what to expect.

Hubert later told me that when he advanced the throttle, the plane very quickly ran off the left side of the runway into the grass. When he made a correction to get back on the runway, he ran as quickly off the other side. By this time, the plane had lurched into the air and thankfully was largely flying itself! Hubert said he looked back into the rear cockpit at Mr. Tinsley. He was just sitting there, cool as a cucumber, exhibiting no reaction whatsoever to the wild events that were taking place.

After I had arrived back home from Vietnam, Hubert wanted me to get checked out in this plane so that we could fly together. I had never flown a tailwheeler before, although I had flown a few civilian planes after getting my license before leaving for Vietnam. Hubert set up the meeting at Downer Airport and I showed up and met Mr. Tinsley, the World War Two fighter pilot. His only instruction was for me to get into the front seat and within a few minutes, someone had turned the prop to get us started. We were soon aimed down the runway, ready for takeoff.

As I advanced the throttle, I detected the tail of the plane commencing a swerve to the right and I immediately corrected it with application of the right rudder pedal. Within a few more seconds the plane was going fast enough for me to push forward on the stick and get the tail of the plane into the air. Moments later, I eased the plane into the air and after climbing straight ahead, turned downwind to make a landing. I flew the plane in the descending half-circle and brought it to a smooth, controlled stop before turning the plane to taxi back toward the take-off end of the runway. Mr. Tinsley could see that I knew what I was doing and said that he had seen enough. With no further comment, the check flight was over.

I think Hubert was disappointed that I had done so well. He would much rather have seen me go through the aerial antics that he had performed when he made <u>his</u> first takeoff. But I had flown probably 800 hours by that time. That amount of experience enabled me to quickly see the need for the corrections that a pilot must make to control the aircraft. I was not surprised at all that I had encountered no problems. Hey, if you're good, you're good. Right?

Over the coming year, we flew together several times, always with the same good results, since I was such a great tailwheel pilot. During that year, I helped Hubert restore a 1946 Piper Cub that he had towed home from Greenville, Mississippi on a flat-bed trailer. When the restoration was complete, we flew it together quite often.

One day we flew thirty miles north to the small airport on the west side of Philadelphia, Mississippi. Later, I looked back at my civilian flight log book and found that prior to this flight, I had made thirty-eight landings in the Cub, all typically good, of course. I was really a hot-shot tailwheel pilot that knew it all by now.

As I made the landing on the north-south runway at Philadelphia that day, there was a pretty stiff left crosswind coming out of the west. I made all of the necessary corrections before finally touching down in the center of the runway. The tail of the plane immediately began drifting to the right so I applied right rudder to correct it. That wasn't enough so I also applied the right brake as well. That wasn't enough, either, and before I knew it, I had run off the left side of the runway! The tall grass there provided enough drag to the tailwheel to enable me to bring the plane to a safe stop.

It turns out that most of us are not quite as bright or as good as we think we are. Let the record show that this talented and qualified tail-wheel pilot had run off the runway on his thirty-ninth landing in the airplane! We are fortunate when we can learn from our mistakes. For too many of us, there is no second chance.

What I learned was something actually quite simple. I didn't know it previously, but tailwheel aircraft have a very low tolerance for crosswind conditions. The second thing is that if you do get into trouble after touchdown in a tailwheeler, simply add the power and get it back into the air. Once there, you will have time enough to think about your options. Sometimes the best one might be to just go somewhere else to land.

My wife always tells me that my self-esteem is too high. It is actually only average for a retired Marine jet pilot. But this time I learned that I wasn't quite as good as I thought I was.

# 37. "I WOULDN'T DO IT AGAIN"

MY FIRST JET FLIGHT INSTRUCTOR, Lieutenant Jim Bouder, was an excellent instructor and a pleasure to fly with. After perhaps a half-dozen flights, he demonstrated a simulated engine-out emergency landing approach for me. It was a maneuver no student would ever perform. Our plane had only one engine and if a student's engine should quit, he was directed to eject rather than try to save the plane. In normal landings, if a landing approach isn't going well, the pilot can always wave off and come back around for another try. If your engine is not running, however, no waveoff is possible. You are committed to ending up on the ground, one way or another.

In Lt. Bouder's demonstration, he did it by the book, aiming for a landing point about a third of the way down the runway. If for some reason he were to have landed short, he would still have been on the runway. If he had been aiming for the normal touch-down point instead, he would have ended up short of the runway with almost certainly disastrous results.

Four years later in 1967, I was an instructor pilot at the same base after completing my first tour in Vietnam. I was flying the T-2A Buckeye, the same type of plane in which I had been trained. I was a young Marine captain with tremendous flying ability like all of the other young pilots. (We had good self-esteem, too). I was now an instructor and was expected to be able to demonstrate the maneuver as it had been demonstrated to me.

Beyond being just a demonstration maneuver, however, it had an obvious practical value as well. One of my Marine captain friends, Jim Pollock, experienced what is called a flameout during an instructional flight while in the vicinity of Starkville, Mississippi. Being competent in the maneuver, Jim glided the plane to a safe landing at an abandoned airfield in that vicinity. After it was repaired, he was assigned to bring it back home by flying it back to NAS Meridian. I would imagine that many of us aggressive young instructor pilots would love to have had the challenge of an engine-out landing like Jim had performed so well. I know I would have.

Besides being utilized in a flameout situation, the maneuver could also be performed as a Precautionary Emergency Landing in some emergency conditions. The engine might still be running but subject to stopping at any time. If the plane could be brought to the commencement point of 4,000 feet of altitude over the runway, the simulated engine-out landing would be performed. Then, if the engine should quit during the maneuver, the pilot could continue the approach as previously practiced and thus save a valuable plane.

I point out, however, that there was no pressure upon the pilots to attempt to land if a true engine-out situation existed. It was the pilot's decision whether to attempt such a landing or not. I remember such an occasion when I was a student there in 1963. After an instructor had climbed to around 20,000 feet following takeoff, the engine slowed to idle rpm and would not respond to attempts to increase it. Several of us students and instructors listened to the discussion of the problem on the base radio in the Operations Room area in the hangar.

After finally determining that the problem was unsolvable, the pilot was asked if he would like to glide back to the field for a Precautionary Emergency Landing. He declined, stating that he would instead eject himself and his student, thus throwing away a perfectly good airplane, in my opinion. The pilot was an older Lieutenant Commander. A younger Marine captain or Navy lieutenant instructor pilot would not have hesitated for an instant to bring the plane back and thus have saved the plane with what I consider minimal risk.

As my flying and instructional skills improved, I would sometimes alter the simulated emergency procedure. Instead of aiming for a point one third of the way down the runway, I would aim for the normal touchdown point, back near the approach end of the runway.

One other factor involved in the procedure was the speed of the plane at touchdown. It had to be just right. Too slow meant the possibility of a stall and crash. Too fast meant floating down the runway until the plane dissipated its excess energy, finally slowing enough to land. To put the plane at the proper landing point at exactly the correct speed was a true challenge in the simulated engine-out maneuver. It had to be flown such that the plane was fast during the last 1,000 feet of the straight-in portion of the approach, thus enabling it to decelerate to the exact correct speed as it touched down at the desired point. As time passed, I became better and better at it.

One day I was flying with Ensign Jim Larkin, one of my regular students. After he had made several good landings I offered to give him a moment's rest. I said, "Jim, I'm going to fly a simulated engine-out approach and put it 'in the box' exactly on speed." He replied, "I know you can do it, Sir. You've shown me before." I impulsively responded, "Well, this time I will put it in the box, on speed, without ever touching the control stick with my hands!"

I climbed to 4,000 feet above the field and called the tower, telling them I was commencing the approach. I then put both hands on the top of my helmet and Jim turned his rear-view mirror so he could see that I was doing what I had said. After 180 degrees of turn I had lost one-half of my original altitude and the approach was going well. I was flying the plane with my knees, the engine still at idle rpm, gear and flaps down, and the speed brakes were extended for the correct simulation of the emergency procedure.

Turning through the 90, I had 90 degrees of turn remaining before being lined up for the straight-in, final portion of the landing. All was looking good and the nose of the aircraft was low to keep the airspeed up. Finally I was rolling wings level with my knees, in the groove, as it was called. I was fast just like I had planned and the plane was slowing as it continued its way toward the touchdown point. My hands had been on my helmet all of the way and Jim kept checking to see if I was cheating. I had to pull back slightly on the stick with my knees as it neared the ground until, finally, "whump" went the touchdown, right on speed exactly where it was supposed to be. It had been a difficult feat, but I had pulled it off.

The flight students were all proud of their instructors and would sometimes brag about what their instructor could do. Jim told me later that he tried telling of my hands-off approach only one time. The other students merely laughed at his obvious exaggeration and gave it no serious consideration.

As for me, granted, I was good enough to do it. But it was still tempting fate. I know one thing for sure. I wouldn't do it again. (And I quickly caution all of you young pilots to <u>not</u> try repeating this!)

# 38. FLYING THE "HUMMER"

I FLEW SEVERAL FAMOUS PLANES during my 20-year Marine Corps career but the military version of the DC-3 was probably the most famous and widely known of them all. It first flew in the early 1930's as the DC-1. Built by the Douglas Aircraft Corporation, it quickly ran through the DC-2 version before settling into large-scale production as the DC-3. I have read that it was the first airplane used by the airline industry that actually made a profit.

Before the end of the Second World War, there had been thousands made and it served in all theaters of the war as the C-47. If you've seen film clips of paratroopers jumping from planes into France on D-Day in 1944, they were jumping from C-47's. It's Navy and Marine Corps designation was the R4D and it was affectionately called the "Hummer," I suppose because it just seemed to hum along. Occasionally I hear one go over, and I can still recognize the unique droning hum of its two nine-cylinder engines without even looking up.

I was checked out in the plane in early 1970 at the Danang air base in Vietnam. I had been flying A-4's but pilots were also needed to fly the cargo missions up and down the coast of Vietnam. The plane was also used for night flare drop missions in support of our ground troops.

I still remember my first training flight with Major Jim Pleasants as my instructor pilot. Despite the solid overcast, we launched up through the clouds and performed the training maneuvers up in the bright sunlight. Finally, Major Pleasants showed me how to "feather" an engine. That consists of shutting the engine down and actuating a motor that turns the propeller blades so they will present the lowest possible drag in the airstream. If an engine loses power, this is an important thing to do because the airplane is now flying on one engine and the drag must be minimized as much as possible.

*The author with a friend and the R4D "Hummer"*

Unfortunately, Major Pleasants could not then show me how to un-feather it! Some malfunction was preventing the blades from returning to their normal position. We now found ourselves flying above the overcast in a true emergency situation with only one working engine! However, Major Pleasants did a great job of returning down through the clouds and executed a flawless ground-controlled approach (GCA) to a safe landing.

My second training flight was with another instructor pilot. After allowing me to make several take-offs and landings, he said, "Let me show you what this plane can do." He then lined up for takeoff, and after checking the engines, pulled one engine back to idle and made a takeoff using only one engine! The plane barely labored into the air. But it made it. It was an amazing feat and one that I would never have thought possible for the plane, having a design and powerplant from the 1930's.

There's not much to say about flying cargo missions up and down the length of South Vietnam. It was still fun to do. And occasionally we would fly over to Ubon or Udorn, Thailand where the Air Force had its large bases for the F-4's and F-105's. Our more interesting missions were the flare-drop missions.

For those missions, the large door on the left side of the plane was removed and perhaps a few dozen or so flares were loaded aboard. Each flare consisted of a tube about four feet long and maybe eight inches in diameter. When thrown out the large open door by our crewmembers back there, a parachute would open and the brilliant flare would ignite. A great deal of illumination would then be provided as the flare floated slowly to the ground.

These flares were used when a ground unit was either being attacked or if they felt that an attack was imminent. We didn't have planes on airborne alert. Instead, we would launch when a call came in requesting our illumination services. The crewmembers would know when they were on standby for such flights, thus ensuring their readiness and keeping them from drinking at the club on their night of standby duty.

One night I was at the movie, if it can be called that. Our movies were projected onto a screen set up in a large room for the evening's show. Near the end of the movie, a call came over the PA system, "Captain Gibson, report to the flight line." My hootch-mate Jess (we lived in crude houses that were called hootches) drove me down to the flight line in a jeep.

It was a dark, overcast night and a light rain was falling. As we pulled out onto the flight line, the airplane sat there in the dim light from the hangars with both engines already running. The "chuka-chuka-chuka" of the two big, idling, radial engines added to the ominous air about the scene. I hurried from the jeep's right seat, climbed aboard, took my pilot's seat, and we launched off into the gloom. My hootchmate told me the next day, "It looked like a scene out of World War Two."

Once up over the overcast, we had no ground reference whatsoever. We were navigating solely by instruments from the ground stations. We made radio contact with the unit needing support and maneuvered until they heard us overhead. We dropped a flare for reference and they directed us closer. Finally, we had their location pinpointed and could drop the flares upon request by reference to our navigation instruments. We seemed to stay up there forever that night, taking turns flying the plane. When we finally landed back at Danang, the first light of the new day was slipping into the eastern sky. It had been a long night. Hopefully we kept some Marines from being killed that night.

The last observation about flying the Hummer is that heretofore I had flown only single-seat jet aircraft. It was quite a surprise to experience the sociability involved when you not only had another pilot sitting beside you, but that as soon as the gear and flaps were up, a sergeant was handing you a cup of coffee.

Believe me, it was a different kind of flying!

# 39. THE GREAT SANTINI

It has been over forty years but I have never forgotten that night. I had played bridge for many years but had never seen the cards go so one-sided for an entire evening. I don't know if my partner and I took the bid for even a single time. Yet, we won by some 3,500 points! It was the night I played bridge with "The Great Santini."

It was the summer of 1970 during my second tour of duty in Vietnam as a Marine Corps attack pilot. I specify that for those who might not know the difference. If I had possessed a measure of God within my being, I might have qualified to have been a fighter pilot. But I was just a normal, everyday kind of guy that could only dream of the things that real fighter pilots do when they are in the air. (Or at least what they say they do). Granted, I flew several types of fighter planes over the years. But anyone can just fly a plane. It's another thing entirely to actually be a fighter pilot who could hope to meet and blast his enemy from the sky and return to Earth and revel in the glory of it all!

But I knew my place in the world. I was just a mere attack pilot who eventually accumulated some 250 combat missions in the best jet attack aircraft the Marine Corps ever had, the A-4 Skyhawk. And for the record, I was a qualified nuclear delivery pilot in that little single-seater, single-engine jet plane. If World War III had ever occurred, The Great Santini may have shot down a dozen Migs, but the enemy would sure as hell have known I had been there when the dust settled. And I would have been first in line requesting to be put on the schedule, just as he would have. I never knew but one Marine pilot that would not have done the same. But that is another story.

I must point out at the outset that I did not know at the time that I was playing bridge with The Great Santini, and for that matter, had never heard of him. And I would not realize it until over thirty-five years later when I happened across an article about Pat Conroy, the author of *The Great Santini*, a book about his greater-than-life father. If you haven't read it, do so.

And it is less a book about the military than what it is like trying to live with the head of a family that is the most egotistical and overbearing Marine that ever lived. Better yet, see the movie of the same name, starring Robert Duvall. For a primer, see some excerpts on YouTube. The article I read identified Pat Conroy as the author of the book and showed a picture of his father, the great man himself, in his dress white uniform, resplendent with all of his medals. When I saw it, I exclaimed to myself, "My goodness! That's the man I played bridge with in Vietnam those many years ago!"

A measure of how unusual the evening was is that the next day I mailed the scorecard home to my wife, who also played bridge. She could look at it and imagine the carnage that my partner and I had inflicted upon our opponents. And I had recalled the event to others many times over the years, mostly in describing how unfairly the bridge gods had been in giving our opponents the better hand each time. I had never bothered speaking of the reaction of the large colonel who sat on my right for the evening, his face ever more-reddening as the night wore on, or how he finally burst out when he had been "set" for perhaps the fifteenth time.

The evening had commenced harmlessly enough. There were several bridge players at the Danang Air Base that would occasionally while away an evening at play. We didn't play very often and the participants were never the same. On the evening in question, I was paired with a chaplain with whom I had played before. I had never met the lieutenant colonel on my left or the colonel on my right. Their names were unimportant to me and I would not have recalled them a day or two later if asked. It was expected to be just another evening of friendly and stimulating bridge play. Little did we know!

During the opening hands, my partner and I were unable to take the bid and had to be content with playing defense. Surprisingly, we were successful in setting them nearly every time and the scorecard showed a gradual accumulation of points in our favor. Our opponents displayed no unusual behavioral characteristics early on, but as the evening progressed, I noticed the colonel seemed to be more and more agitated. I haven't played in many years but I recall that one has to be philosophical about how the cards happen to fall. Sometimes they go one way and sometimes the other. One has to be content with his lot and do his best with what he is given.

The colonel wasn't buying it, though. "The hell with philosophy!" he must have thought, as he finally angrily stood up, bursting out, "You guys just aren't bidding your hands!" He had had enough. We had played several hours and it was time to quit. So we shut down the cards for the evening and returned to our lonely hootches, having completed one more day of the long year of separation from our families.

Other than writing my wife the next day as described, I never gave the colonel another thought over the years. But seeing the article thirty-five years later, it came into clear focus. After having read the book and seen the movie, I consider myself lucky! If it had happened during the days of old, I may have been challenged to a duel.

And I <u>know</u> how that would have ended!

(Note—I want to emphasize that Colonel Conroy's behavior was totally within normal bounds that evening. My description of his being egotistical and overbearing is taken from the book his son wrote, and from the movie, *The Great Santini*. He was a great Marine and a great American and I have nothing but appreciation and respect for him and his service to our country. It was a great honor to play bridge with this fine man.)

# 40. A TERRIBLE CRASH

I DON'T REMEMBER WHERE WE had been on that March day in 1970, the day the crash occurred. I had been flying various missions in the R4D at the time, and we were returning to the Danang Air Base from somewhere to the south. The Danang airfield had parallel runways in basically north-south directions and was one of the largest air facilities within South Vietnam. The eastern side of the base housed U. S. Air Force units and the Marines were located on the west side of the field. The difference between the two sides was like night and day.

The Marine Corps side had dirt roads (read dusty or muddy) while the roads on the Air Force side were all paved. The Marines lived in tents while the Air Force had air-conditioned buildings. The Marines had few jeeps available while it seemed every Corporal or above in the Air Force had his own jeep.

My description is exaggerated, of course. Also, these conditions may not have continued throughout the years of the U. S. presence in South Vietnam. But they were the impressions I came away with at the time. A small joke had existed for years regarding ground transportation in the Marine Corps. It went, "You can tell the story of the Marine Corps in two words---no wheels!"

As I approached the field from the south I was directed to make a straight-in approach to a landing on the left (western) runway. As I got closer I was further directed to be sure to safely clear some workers at the approach end of the runway. So I passed perhaps sixty feet over these workers, landing slightly "long," but completing an otherwise uneventful landing.

We turned off the end of the runway and taxied southwards back down the west side of the airfield until arriving at our squadron area. We shut the two big propeller engines down, exitted the plane, and began walking toward the hangar. It was then that I saw a large four-engine plane approaching to land on the same runway I had just landed upon. It was a Lockheed Super Constellation EC-121, an easily recognizable plane with its three vertical stabilizers at the tail surfaces.

During the Vietnamese War era, this plane was used in electronic surveillance missions up and down the Chinese and North Vietnamese coasts. A large plane, it had the ability to fly for seeming hours on end. I read that the missions could be up to fourteen hours long. In fact, its reconnaissance missions were so long in duration that they sometimes carried an entire backup crew. One crew could thus rest after a certain number of hours and even sleep if required. We had no idea of what its mission was or where it had been that day. It was just an EC-121 "Super Connie" coming in to land, perhaps three fourths of a mile away from us as it neared the end of the runway.

Then we saw the plane stop its descent as the pilot apparently applied power to level out and even begin to climb, initiating a waveoff of the landing approach. But I noticed something unusual in that not only was the plane beginning a slight climb but it was also beginning a shallow right turn. That was unusual. If the pilot intended to turn downwind, as it was called, normal procedure would have been to climb straight ahead to a safe altitude before commencing his turn.

But the straight-ahead climb wasn't happening. Instead, as the nose continued coming up, the angle of bank kept increasing as well. I told the pilot beside me, "If he goes past thirty degrees angle of bank, there is a problem," because I knew that planes of that size just didn't go around making steep angles of bank. But the bank angle kept increasing as the nose of the plane now began slowly dropping back toward level flight. By now, the airplane was at nearly ninety degrees angle of bank! All of this time we could hear the thundering roar of its engines at full power as the pilot was fighting to regain control of the plane.

It had managed to climb to perhaps four hundred feet, now turned fully crossways to the runways as it plummeted toward the ground, finally crashing into the tops of the hangars on the Air Force side of the runway. We saw pieces flying in all directions as it exploded into smoke and flame.

Peculiarly, because the sound took so long to get to us, the roar of the engines continued for perhaps six or seven seconds after the crash was observed. Finally, the sound of the crash arrived and the roar of the engines was silenced forever.

We later learned that the plane was returning from one of its long surveillance missions somewhere to the north towards China. To make matters even worse, two complete crews were aboard the plane, totaling nearly thirty men. Over twenty of the crewmembers were killed, a catastrophe to lose so many men in a single crash.

Years later I met a Navy pilot who had flown such planes and its missions and I recounted having observed this crash. He remembered the event well and gave some insight to its cause. The plane was making its approach with its number three engine inoperative and the propellers of that engine feathered. The number three engine is the one nearest to the cockpit on the right side of the aircraft. Recall the workers at the end off the runway? They may have been the inadvertent cause of the waveoff. I believe the pilot was higher than usual because of the workers and elected to wave off the approach. He may even have intended to go to the other runway where no obstacles existed.

Having two good engines on the left and only one on the right side probably caused the left wing to be pulled forward due to the asymmetrical thrust of the unbalanced engine situation. The pilot may have applied the throttles too abruptly during the waveoff. If he had applied the power more gradually, there may have been enough time to make the necessary corrections and a dangerous situation might have been avoided. I am not judging the pilot but merely trying to explain what I think caused the crash.

In any event, the plane was carrying over two dozen young men who would much rather have been back home with their families if they could have had their choice. Instead, they were serving their country and its people to the utmost of their abilities, and in the end they gave their all. Our nation has been blessed in each generation to have such men and women, who have been willing to put their lives on the line, chancing the loss of life itself if deemed necessary, in the service of their country.

# 41. U. S. NAVAL TEST PILOT SCHOOL

OF ALL MY STORIES, THIS is the most difficult one for me to write. Never in my life have I undergone such acute pain and disappointment as when I was dropped from this school.

In 1959, three years before I entered the Marine Corps, seven young pilots were selected to be our nation's first astronauts. They were John Glenn, Scott Carpenter, Wally Schirra, Gus Grissom, Alan Shepherd, Gordon Cooper, and Deke Slayton. They were not only pilots from the various military services, but were all graduates of the military test pilot schools as well. Having loved airplanes all of my life and having aspired to be a military pilot some day, these men epitomized what I wanted to become.

After completing my master's degree in mechanical engineering, I earned my commission as a second lieutenant at Quantico, Virginia and went on to complete flight training in jets in 1964. In early 1972, after eight years of flying, I was selected to attend the U. S. Naval Test Pilot School at NAS Patuxent River, Maryland. I arrived there with my family (wife and two children) in June of that year. It was one of the happiest and proudest moments of my life as I met my fellow prospective test pilots and commenced the training.

I initially did well in both academics and in flying the various aircraft maintained by the school. I remember writing my first report on evaluation of the flight control system of one of the planes. We had been told that if we received a grade of C to not be concerned. It actually meant that the overall evaluation and report was well done and satisfactory. I received a grade of C so I suppose I was parring the course. As the months went by I did some things well and other things not as well. But another factor was creeping up on me beyond my ability to perceive.

When our class first commenced, the class ahead of us was nearing completion and had a few suggestions and words of wisdom for us. The only one I remember was, "Whatever you do, don't let Mr. Moore get against you. He can really hurt you," or words to that effect. Mr. Moore was a civilian, in his mid-fifties, a fairly large man and an ex-Marine pilot who had flown combat missions during the Korean conflict. I paid it no mind. I was fairly easy to get along with and didn't go out of my way to arouse ill feelings from others. Besides, I had flown my share of combat missions, too.

Mr. Moore was a very competent math and aerodynamics instructor who taught most of the academic courses at the school. Although a little withdrawn and humorless, he still inspired respect as far as I was concerned. But about half-way through the nine-month school, I began picking up vibes that he didn't like me very much for some reason. Let me give you an objective view.

One day in the aerodynamics class, Mr. Moore used several equations including what was called "The Heaviside Equation." The class ended a few minutes later and I stood waiting to ask a question about the equation as he left the podium. Mr. Moore brushed me aside without even looking at me, saying "You'll have to ask Mr. Heaviside about that." Never mind that Mr. Heaviside had been dead for nearly fifty years; there was no way I could have asked him anyway.

I stood there as Mr. Moore walked on by as another class member, Walt Honour, asked him a question from his desk. Mr. Moore said, "Sure, Walt, it goes like this," as he bent over him, practically putting his arm around his shoulder, showing him how to work the problem. I went upstairs to the room designated as our home room while at the school. Within a few minutes, another student, Mike Williams, entered the room, walked over to me and said, "I saw what happened, Larry, and if I were you I would really be mad." I wasn't mad. I was just dejected to have been so ill-treated while trying so hard in the school.

Not long after that I received a D-minus on the flight evaluation of a T-38 aircraft I had flown. During the course of the flight I had overstressed the plane by a tenth of a "g" (!) and had recorded the value in my report. Commander Doug Dunbar graded the report and told me that a test pilot must always know exactly where he is in relation to the aircraft's capabilities and limitations and that I therefore merited the low grade. For the record, another student, a U. S. Army pilot, also over-stressed a T-28 in a similar manner, so it wasn't like it never happened.

Mr. Moore may have heard about the low grade on my flight report. I can now envision him like a shark knifing silently through the water toward his intended and unsuspecting victim. A few days later he gave a really difficult aerodynamics exam just before the lunch hour. We students later discussed its unusual difficulty. It was on a Friday in late November.

Later that afternoon, the Commander of the Test Pilot School, a Navy captain whose name I do not recall, called me into his office. The gist of it was, "Well, Major Gibson, You've been having a few difficulties but have managed to hang in there. But this afternoon Mr. Moore brought me your test paper from an examination earlier today, and I must say it was pretty bad. I am going to have to remove you from the course of instruction." My heart sank as I made my way home. It truly was the most acute disappointment of my life, and I've had a few other bad ones for reference.

Within a few days our family had moved away from the base to Virginia, near Washington, DC, where I served for nearly four years at Headquarters, Marine Corps. It was a tremendous let-down to fly a desk all week after testing high-performance jet aircraft.

Some six months later I saw my friend Mike Williams again, who had managed to complete the course successfully. During the conversation, I mentioned the difficult exam that Mr. Moore had given us on the day I was dropped. I asked how the remainder of the class had done.

Jim looked me in the eye and said, "Larry, Mr. Moore never did give that exam back to us."

# 42. COLONEL DON ANDERSON

I was assigned to Headquarters, Marine Corps for three and a half years. During that time I had four bosses who were head of the AAZ Branch within the Aviation Division, which was headed by a major general. There were five sections within AAZ and for most of my tour of duty, I was the sole officer in AAZ-5. I was responsible for flight pay issues and medical qualifications for aviation officers and any aviation board action that might come to Headquarters from anywhere in the world.

It hadn't always been that way. When I was first assigned to AAZ-5, there were two other officers and a very capable sergeant already in the section. One was a lieutenant colonel and the other a very competent major who was senior to me. So I wasn't going to shine in that environment. I was also going through marital problems at the time, which didn't help, either.

My first boss, Colonel Blaha, gave me a low rating on my first fitness report and when I discussed it with him, had the gall to lie to me by saying, "I consider you to be in the upper 20 % of all Marine Corps majors." Fortunately, he was my boss for less than a year and was replaced by Colonel Don Anderson.

Colonel Anderson was a tall and slender officer from a fighter pilot background. He was from somewhere out west and had a cowboy air about him, which he did not mind cultivating. I recall his references to rodeos and he may have even participated in them at one time. I recall him once saying his rodeo "moniker" was Belt Buckle, as in, "Our next bronco buster is Belt Buckle, hailing from -- etc." I believe this was spoken in jest, but it fit the persona he often projected.

The colonel was highly competent with a dry, laconic wit that only a cowboy turned fighter pilot could possess. On many afternoons, after the civilians had left at 4:30, he would regale his staff of officers with various tales, some of which may not have been true, but you could never tell. Even the ones that were true came out in a highly entertaining and sometimes earthy manner. I remember him saying once, "Anyone that says you can't get too much of a good thing has never shoveled manure on a hot summer day!"

During the summers, it was sometimes warm in our offices and after a hard day's office work, one might look a little wilted. Military personnel were required to wear their uniforms one day per week. That day was called CRUD Day, meaning "Commandant requires uniform day." The colonel would sometimes do a cute trick at around 4:30. He would change into a fresh uniform shirt and go down to the general's office looking crisp and sharp and shoot the bull for a few minutes with the higher-ups.

I was reminded of reading about General MacArthur when he was in the Philippines in the 1930's. They had no air conditioning in Manila, I'm sure, and I read that he would go through perhaps three or four uniforms per day to keep looking really sharp throughout the day. I don't know if the colonel was cognizant of that fact, but he was emulating it at least to some degree.

After a short time, the lieutenant colonel in AAZ-5 left, leaving me, Major Ken Town, and the proficient sergeant working in the section. I stress again that Ken was a very competent and hard-working staff officer, leaving very little for me to do. And I continued to receive low fitness report marks from Colonel Anderson.

A word about car pools is in order regarding my years of assignment to Headquarters. I lived 25 miles down I-95 in a bedroom community named Dale City. Numerous other officers also lived there, and everyone was in a car pool of some sort. For a long time, I rode with Lieutenant Colonel Bob Peterson, a very competent staff officer from AAP, another branch within the Aviation Division.

Lieutenant Colonel Peterson liked to be the first officer to get there each morning and get to be the one to unlock the office doors. That idiosyncrasy was coupled with the common behavior of all of the staff officers in that they would never leave before at least 5:30, thereby displaying their great work ethic and willingness to work overtime for the Corps. No one wanted to leave early and appear to be a non-hacker.

A year and a half later, Ken received orders to leave Headquarters at about the same time that my car pool friend received his. So here is what I did. I went in to see Colonel Anderson and told him that I did not feel that I had been properly evaluated while working behind Major Town. I said, "I don't want you to replace Ken in AAZ-5. I want to do the entire job myself so you can see what I can do." I added, "And I've joined a new car pool and from now on I'm leaving at 4:30 with the civilians." He responded, "I don't care what time you leave. Just get the job done." I emphasize that the official work day ended at 4:30 for everyone. It was just that no officer wanted to be seen leaving early. So you can imagine what it looked like when I began leaving at the same time as the civilians!

Unfortunately, the sergeant in AAZ-5 was so competent that he was transferred to the general's office and I received a young, black Lance Corporal in his place. He was unusually non-communicative in the office and I soon heard that he was getting into trouble back in his barracks. When I took this information to the Colonel, he wisely said, "Get rid of him. That's the kind of guy that comes in some Monday morning and sprays the office with an M-16!"

He was replaced by another clerk that was able to do the job and communicate at the same time. I may have had to eat my lunch of sandwiches while working at my desk, and I may have been handicapped by a less-experienced clerk, but I got the job done. Subsequent fitness reports from the colonel were at least average for what my peers were getting. But the damage had already been done and I realized my chances for promotion to the next rank were very slim.

While head of the AAZ Branch, Colonel Anderson came up for promotion to brigadier general. One Friday afternoon, as he was holding court with his story-telling sessions, an officer asked him if he thought he would be promoted. He unhesitatingly said, "No way! I'm not on the team. There is no way that I will be promoted. You have to have a well-placed and highly effective sponsor to get promoted to that rank."

I didn't think much about it at the time, but later, in the course of my duties, I was required to review the colonel's Officer Qualification Jacket for some reason. I couldn't help seeing the high level of fitness reports that he had received while head of AAZ. The head of the Aviation Division, General Fris, had singled him out as the best of approximately ten colonels on his staff. He emphasized that Colonel Anderson was not a yes man and would tell you like it was without trying to sugar coat or soften anything. General Fris highly recommended Colonel Anderson for promotion to general.

But it was not to be. When the results came out, it was as the colonel had predicted. Even with the greatest of fitness reports while in competition with the best staff officers of the rank of colonel in the Marine Corps, he still was not promoted. Like the colonel had said, he wasn't on the team. He understood the process and was not bitter about it.

When Colonel Anderson left, the senior lieutenant colonel in AAZ took over for a month or so before the next colonel arrived. Not long after that, a large project came to the branch and he gave me the assignment. It didn't relate to my normal duties and I tried to get out of doing it. But he responded, "Well, you're the one that leaves early every day so you must not have enough to do." You can't win! If you don't play the game and stay at your desk until 5:30, you must not be doing all you can for the Corps! So, I did the additional assignment.

My last boss at Headquarters was Colonel Paul German, about whom I have written in another story. Colonel German had been the Chief of Staff for the general's office before coming to AAZ and was well acquainted with its duties. I enjoyed working for Colonel German more than any of the previous bosses, and for the record, he also gave me very good fitness report marks.

I don't mean to brag, because I've told you that I had received weak marks before. But I think it is worth giving you a direct quote from one of Colonel German's evaluations of my performance of duties. He began my final report by writing, "Major Gibson's research, analysis, and completed staff work are still the most thorough in the Branch." Considering that the comment was made in a branch of some ten majors and lieutenant colonels, it reflected well on the quality of work that I was doing. And, if I might add, that was just me doing the work where there had once been three officers working. Enough said.

I will finish this story with one told by Colonel Anderson one Friday afternoon before we secured for the weekend. I will paraphrase the story as I remember him telling it.

"Years ago when I was a young lieutenant, I happened to find myself in an elevator in the pentagon with a navy captain. I spoke to him, saying, 'Captain, I see that you have received the Silver Star. Would you mind telling me what you did to receive that medal?' He responded":

'I received that medal following the landings by the Marines at Inchon, South Korea in 1950 during the Korean War. When General MacArthur heard of the success of the invasion, he turned to a staff officer and said, "I want the captain of every ship participating in this landing to receive the Silver Star!" The staff officer took the general's request to the navy and I was given the task of gathering the required information.

'Finally, the day arrived when I shepherded the officers into a large room and the general went down the line pinning the Silver Star medals upon their chests. I happened to be standing near the end of the line and the next thing I knew, the general was pinning one on me! I tried to stop him, saying, "But sir, I didn't do anything to deserve this medal." The general then said, "I don't want to hear any of your modesty, Lieutenant, you earned this medal and I am going to see that you receive it!"

'Later, after the general and most of his staff had left, I approached one of the colonels remaining behind and asked, "How am I ever going to explain to anyone what I did to receive this medal?" The staff officer responded, "Lieutenant, believe me, when you read your citation, you will <u>know</u> why you received the Silver Star!"'

# 43. "I'M NOT ASKING YOU WHAT YOU THINK, MAJOR"

My last boss at Headquarters, Marine Corps, was Colonel Paul German, a good-natured, likable, methodical, and quiet-spoken man. He had been the Chief of Staff down in the general's office before becoming the head of AAZ, where I worked. AAZ usually had about eight to ten officers and I was the only officer in the smallest section, AAZ-5. When I had first been assigned there, two other officers were also in the section, but it was down to just me and a Corporal by the time Colonel German took over.

I was responsible for three subject areas within headquarters. They were qualification for flight pay, medical qualifications for pilots, and any board action regarding Marine Corps pilots, occurring anywhere in the world. The subject of proficiency flying also came under my cognizance but there was generally little to do with that subject.

Pilots were normally required to fly a minimum of one hundred hours per year. The purpose is quite obvious. Flying military aircraft is something that must be regularly practiced in order to maintain the necessary skills. It wouldn't make much sense to train a pilot at great expense and then allow him to lose those skills through inactivity.

Attainment of these flight hours was easy to accomplish when pilots were assigned to military aviation units. However, pilots were sometimes assigned to desk jobs where no tactical aviation units were available. In these instances, the Proficiency Flying Program was utilized for all pilots below the rank of colonel. These pilots then flew trainer-type aircraft to maintain their basic flying skills. Presumably, most colonels and generals would not normally return to flight assignments upon leaving their desk jobs. Or if they did, they had flown for so many years that the 100-hour requirement was waived.

I point out, however, that nearly all pilots wanted to fly and would have preferred the waiver did not exist. And that is what brought about a potentially embarrassing incident involving Colonel German and myself.

Some friend of the colonel had called him and wanted to be able to fly in the Proficiency Flying Program, despite being in an assignment and of a rank that would preclude his participation. Colonel German called me into his office and asked me to compose a letter authorizing the officer's request. After reviewing the particulars, I went back to the colonel and told him that it could not be authorized for the reasons stated above.

The colonel didn't want to disappoint his friend and asked me to take a more in-depth look to see if anything could be done. After doing so, I again told the colonel that it would be a violation of the regulations. He then asked me for a third time to see if a thorough review might find some loophole.

After a diligent search and a thorough appraisal of the situation, I had to make yet another trip to the colonel, telling him, "Colonel, I don't think we will be able to permit this officer to fly in his current assignment." Colonel German then looked up to me from his desk and pointedly said, "I'm not asking you what you think, Major. I'm telling you what to write!" As any fine staff officer would do, I said, "Yes, sir," and returned to my office and wrote the letter of authorization.

After composing the letter for the colonel's signature, I forgot the matter and life went on. But one afternoon a few weeks later, Colonel German called me into his office. He said, "Larry, the Assistant Commandant of the Marine Corps has asked that I come to his office in regard to that letter we sent about proficiency flying. I need for you to go with me." So off we went to see the wizard, so to speak.

The Assistant Commandant was General Leslie E. Brown, a truly fine officer of four-star rank. I had served under the general when we were flying A-4's at Chu Lai, South Vietnam in 1966. He was a colonel then and the Commanding Officer of Marine Air Group Twelve (MAG-12). Not that he would remember it, of course, but I had a friend take a picture of us in our flight gear immediately upon return from our separate flights. Colonel German and I proceeded up a few flights of steps and made our way to his office.

*The author with the MAG-12 Group Commander, Colonel Leslie E. Brown*

I remind the reader that a four-star general is four ranks higher than a bird colonel, a fact of which I'm sure Colonel German was very much aware. General Brown welcomed us into his office and remained standing as he spoke. He was very kind in how he phrased his question, saying something like, "I see where General _____ is engaging in proficiency flying. I didn't realize he would be able to do this in his current assignment. What can you tell me about it?"

Before Colonel German could speak, I said, "General, I'm the one that drafted that letter and I believe I may have made a mistake." General Brown graciously responded, "Well, how about the two of you review this matter and be sure that it meets the appropriate regulations for me."

It was all said in a low-key and soft manner, allowing Colonel German and me to extricate ourselves with a minimum of loss of face. We assured him that we would give it our immediate attention. The General excused us, and once we were out of his office, Colonel German turned to me and said, with an expression of relief, "Well, Larry, you sure were right about that one!"

# 44. A FLIGHT STUDENT
# WEARING GLASSES

DURING MY THREE AND A half years at Headquarters, Marine Corps (HQMC), my little office (AAZ-5) dealt with medical qualifications and flight pay matters for officer flight personnel. If any Marine pilot had difficulty meeting some particular medical requirement, he could request a waiver if he felt that he could perform satisfactorily in spite of his apparent shortcoming. The waiver had to be submitted via the chain of command and would ultimately arrive on my desk after endorsement by The Chief, Bureau of Medicine and Surgery (BUMED), within the Department of the Navy.

Meanwhile, he would be kept in a 90-day approved flight status while the waiver request worked its way through the system. These requests were usually from aviators found to be technically overweight, but who thought their present weight should be considered acceptable. The requests had to be accompanied by two photos in gym trunks, one from the front and the other from the side, showing the pilot from head to toe in each photo.

For Marine Corps personnel, BUMED would put a cursory endorsement upon such requests and forward them to the Commandant of the Marine Corps (CMC) for final decision. BUMED's endorsement might say, in effect, "The Chief, Bureau of Medicine and Surgery interposes no objection to this request and defers to Headquarters, Marine Corps for final decision regarding this matter."

Usually if someone cared enough to get the pictures taken and go through the process, their health and capabilities at this higher weight were probably satisfactory and I would recommend to my boss that it be approved. In fact, I would have the form letter already typed and send it in for his signature with a short note explaining why I felt it should be approved. The CMC letter authorizing the waiver would then establish his new maximum weight to be whatever it had been on the day of the physical exam that had started the whole process.

This procedure was very sensible and allowed judgment to exist and prevented aircrew members from being held hostage to some seemingly arbitrary height/weight chart. After all, some people are larger-boned than others and would thus weigh more whether they had much fat on them or not.

A major from the ground side of the house at Headquarters was in my carpool for a while. His assignment happened to be similar to mine, regarding medical qualifications for ground officers, although we had never discussed it. However, in 1975 General Louis Wilson became the new Commandant of the Marine Corps. A tall and slender Marine, General Wilson wanted all of his Marines to be lean, and presumably mean as well. My counterpart related to me how it was having an adverse effect on many ground career Marines.

The problem was that the ground side of the house did not entertain the idea of medical waivers. Perhaps before this time the problem had just been ignored. But I was now told by my carpool friend of the difficulties that many ground officers (and enlisted as well) were encountering because they were suddenly considered to be overweight. Many of them were just big, large-boned, strong men whose weight did not conform to the standards shown on the chart. I explained how we dealt with this matter on the aviation side of the house, but I don't think his bosses ever agreed with this practical and proper conclusion of how to deal with it.

The ultimate case of the application of judgment regarding waivers occurred around 1975 or 1976 as I neared the end of my Headquarters tour. A young lieutenant was applying for flight training but he had a medical condition that appeared to preclude him from being accepted. The lieutenant wore glasses! However, upon reading his application and reviewing his qualifications, I found that he had his commercial pilot's license, was instrument-qualified, and had over two hundred hours of flight time.

I had never heard of an applicant being accepted for flight training who was already wearing glasses. However, provision existed for designated, qualified pilots to remain in a flying status if their eyes deteriorated later in their career. The only restriction was that these pilots could not operate from aircraft carriers.

This restriction existed because of the violence of the arrested landings and being catapulted from the ship. For incoming students, it was generally considered not to be worth the risk to begin the training process with someone who already wore glasses. Training military pilots, perhaps more so for the Navy and Marine Corps, was very expensive and they wanted to have the students to at least begin their training with no apparent problems regarding qualification.

As I considered the waiver request, I could see that this student almost certainly posed no threat of failing to make the grade. It appeared to be a very safe bet that he would satisfactorily complete the program. And, upon graduation, he, like many other Naval Aviators, would simply be a qualified pilot who happened to wear glasses but was still qualified for nearly all existing assignments.

This time I didn't draft the letter first and then send it to my boss, Colonel German, for his signature. I first went to his office and discussed it with him, explaining my rationale for the proposed favorable response to the young lieutenant's request. The colonel immediately concurred, and the letter was prepared and sent back through the chain of command.

I never heard more about it, but at some time during the following months, a lieutenant probably showed up at NAS Pensacola for ground school, wearing glasses. I have always liked to think that this epitomized the manner in which requests for waiver should be considered. Instead of a precise cookie-cutter mold for all, some judgment and consideration should be given to maximize the opportunity for each individual to serve in his or her most effective capacity.

I am confident the young man became a qualified pilot and served well in the years following his designation as a Naval Aviator. It would be interesting to know for sure. Maybe he will read this humble literary effort and recognize himself.

# 45. "LAUNCH THE SERGEANTS"

APPROXIMATELY FIFTEEN HUNDRED OF MY 5,600 flight hours were flown in tactical jet aircraft. Generally, the term "tactical jet" means the plane is either used to fight other aircraft or to attack ground targets. Those aircraft often carry only a pilot, or if another person is present, he or she is another aviation officer with a high degree of training to assist in performance of the aircraft's mission.

Other types of planes, however, often carried enlisted men who were referred to as enlisted aircrewmembers. They may also have had a lot of specific training, but different from the officers mentioned above. Sometimes these crewmembers assisted in maintenance of the planes and often became very familiar with their operation. The highest level of an example refers to those crewmembers that were qualified to start up the engines for various maintenance purposes. In some cases, they may have even been qualified to taxi the plane from one position on the field to another.

On some missions in cargo planes, a crewmember might occasionally ride in the cockpit as the plane droned along slowly from one point to another. By doing so, they could gradually acquire quite a bit of knowledge about operation of the aircraft as it traversed the airways, or just about its normal flight procedures.

One dark night around 1977 at MCAS Iwakuni, Japan, two crewmembers arrived at the flight line at around midnight and proceeded to an R4D aircraft. The R4D was affectionately called the Hummer and I have previously written about some of my experiences in that plane. It was a twin-engine, propeller-driven plane that had been named the DC-3 in its previous civilian life before and after World War II. It was a rather

167

large tailwheel type of aircraft and, in some landing and takeoff situations, could be difficult to fly.

If someone had witnessed the arrival of the two crewmembers and had seen them enter the aircraft, they may not have been suspicious. They would have recognized them as qualified crewmembers and no alarm would have been sounded. They would then have appeared to be doing various tasks around the outside and inside of the plane. The observers, if any existed, might not have even been surprised when, after several minutes, the engines were started.

After several more minutes, the two crewmembers called Iwakuni Ground Control for clearance to taxi the plane to another position on the field. Ground Control graciously provided the clearance. Such a request was not particularly unusual as they assumed it was for some maintenance reason. Thus, after deft applications of "power" to the two large radial engines, the plane began slowly moving from its familiar position on the squadron's flight line.

It happened to not only be a very dark night; it was also one of bad weather and low cloud ceilings hovered over the surrounding area. The plane, meanwhile, continued to methodically taxi along the taxiway until nearing the takeoff end of the runway. There, the plane stopped and sat for several minutes. Finally, the engines were run to high speed as though they were being checked for some reason.

Then, surprisingly to the tower personnel, who were probably the only ones awake in the area, the aircraft turned onto the runway and, without proper clearance, and with no qualified pilot aboard, began roaring down the runway as if to take off!

And, in fact, it did take off! Away it climbed into the black overcast of the night, the sounds of the powerful engines growing gradually fainter as it disappeared into the overcast. This had probably happened at other times over the course of aviation history, but for all practical purposes, it was an unprecedented event!

Although I don't know all of the details of what occurred over the next few hours, the general proceedings later became commonly known. It turned out that the two would-be pilots were both sergeants and assigned as aircrewmembers for this particular aircraft.

The two sergeants not only flew the plane. They flew it all the way to Okinawa, hundreds of miles away across the Pacific Ocean, in the dark of night. I later heard that the authorities had finally made radio contact with them. Upon their arrival over Kadena Air Base in Okinawa, they were directed to make a gear-up landing because of the lesser risk involved for the two sergeants. The sergeants declined the offer, however, and proceeded to make what must have been a passable landing. They then surrendered into the hands of the local authorities at the Kadena Air Base.

Even if this had occurred in the middle of the afternoon on a beautiful day, it would still have been an astonishing event. Its accomplishment under such adverse conditions merited admiration from anyone familiar with the challenges that were overcome.

Thereafter, whenever a mission was being considered under weather conditions which might prevent launch of the aircraft involved, the cry would go up among the pilots who were tasked with launching into such unfavorable conditions, "Launch the Sergeants!"

# 46. THE BOSTON MARATHON AND ROSIE RUIZ

The Marine Corps is notorious for its fighting spirit and the toughness of its fighting forces. One of the activities that contribute to this toughness is what is called the Quarterly Physical Fitness Test (PFT). A PFT is performed by all personnel within each Marine Corps unit four times per year. The three events comprising the PFT are chin-ups, sit-ups (also called crunches), and a three-mile run. The latter events are timed events and the Marine receives a maximum score for performing twenty chin-ups, one hundred crunches in two minutes or less, and running the three miles in eighteen minutes or less.

It is not particularly difficult to merely pass the PFT for individuals in fairly good physical condition, but to make the maximum score one has to be in unusually good overall condition. I never made the maximum score until my latter years in the Marine Corps. That achievement was due to my having become a marathon runner.

In the spring of 1978, the Marines within our training squadron at NAS Meridian conducted the PFT as per usual and my score was probably just average as I was doing no unusual training at the time. After the event, Captain Jim Collins suggested that some of us consider running the Marine Corps Marathon in November of that year. Jim had run it the previous fall and was willing to provide suggestions regarding training for the event. A few of us took him up on it and began training for the marathon that would be conducted some seven months later.

I remember asking him about the speed at which we should run during the training. He said, "Run at a speed at which you could be carrying on a conversation with a fellow runner." That puzzled me as I would never have thought of being able to talk while running. The common perception is that one would be out of breath and be unable to do so. I eventually learned that he was right. In fact, there were several marathons where I would run the entire distance of 26.2 miles while conversing with another runner.

The Marine Corps birthday is on November 10th and the marathon was held in Washington, DC on the Saturday nearest that date. The Marine Corps Iwo Jima Memorial was used as both the starting and ending points for the run. I found that the first twelve miles or so passed fairly easily. It then became tougher at around fifteen miles, and it became very difficult after around twenty miles.

I didn't do particularly well on this first attempt but I completed it, which was the main goal. But on each subsequent marathon, I completed the run in less time than the previous one. By early 1980 I had accomplished the qualifying time for participation in the Boston Marathon. At the time, I was over 40 years of age and the qualifying time was 3:10 (three hours and ten minutes or less). My qualifying time was 3:05.

I flew one of the squadron training planes to the event, landing at nearby NAS South Weymouth. A flight student accompanied me and a navigation training flight was conducted during the flight there and also during the return. The student was Marine Lieutenant Charles (Chuck) Moseley, who later became a member of the Blue Angels Flight Demonstration Team. Chuck positioned himself near the finish line and told me later of seeing not only me complete the run, but another instructor with whom he also had flown when at Pensacola.

Running such a long distance requires that the athlete pace himself (or herself). I emphasize the point about herself because the average woman's time that day at Boston was one minute faster than my time of 3:14. The point of pacing is that a person could always run faster at any given time during the race, but it might result in an overall longer time to complete the run. One has to run at the pace that will enable the race to be completed in the minimum time, and still not have unused energy remaining at the end of the race. I can honestly say that I did my absolute best in every marathon run I ever ran. I used all I had every time.

The day of the Boston Marathon in April of 1980 was a beautiful one although the temperature was a little too high, probably in the mid-sixties. The uninitiated would think that this temperature would be ideal, but it is much too warm. Running causes the body to heat up and temperatures in the forties are preferred.

Because of my late application to participate, I had the second-highest registration number issued for the race. As the commencement time for the race approached, I took my place at the very rear of the group of runners. I heard the gun fire, signaling the beginning of the race, but it took over two minutes for us at the rear to get to the starting line. And due to the large number of runners involved, it took over an hour before I could run unimpeded.

In all of my previous marathons, spectators had been nearly non-existent. Not so at Boston! We ran through at least a half-dozen small towns with the crowds lining the roads and even on the roads forming narrow lanes through which the runners had to pass. Sometimes the running lane was so narrow that we could run only two-abreast.

Many people offered water, Gatorade, and even slices of oranges as we ran by them. In some cases, people had their lawn sprinklers running and one could run to the side for a cooling spray of water. I had never seen a marathon like it before and never would again.

Finally, as we entered the city of Boston, the crowds were even larger, cheering the runners on. Sometimes a person would be holding a sign saying, "Two more miles," or the like. As we entered downtown Boston, the crowds were even louder as the sounds echoed off the buildings. And finally, mercifully I might add, the finish line was in sight.

I completed the run in 3 hours and 14 minutes, finishing number 2,559th of some 9,000 runners. The important thing was not the particular time or that I finished in a given position. The Boston Marathon is the Mecca of the running world and the most prestigious of the marathons run, probably in the world. The important thing is that I had been able to participate in this marathon as a qualified runner and that I had completed it successfully. And, I had done my best, of course.

After crossing the finish line, the runners were directed to a parking garage under one of the adjacent tall buildings. As I entered the large garage I saw the winner, Bill Rogers (his fourth win), receiving an award on a nearby stage. He had completed far enough ahead of me to have already had his shower and to be comfortably dressed.

Later, I was sitting on the edge of the sidewalk waiting for a ride with a Navy friend who had also run the event. We were both totally beat, of course. Suddenly we saw a young lady runner walking along the sidewalk towards us. She was wearing the traditional crown of olive leaves that the winners were awarded. I said to my friend, "That must be the woman that won the women's portion of the event." Looking at her, he said, "It doesn't look like she has even been running to me!"

It turned out that he was right. She had commenced the run in the proper fashion, but had then exited the run and taken a cab to a point a mile or so from the finish line. At the appropriate time, she had re-entered the race, enabling her to come in as the first place winner among the women. I saw her crossing the finish line later that night on one of the Boston TV stations. She faked it beautifully as she imitated someone barely able to finish the run. The crowd was going wild in appreciation of the first woman to complete the race. But I could see what I had seen earlier on the sidewalk. She was much too voluptuous to be a serious runner.

The officials were faced with a dilemma. They realized from her appearance that she had cheated. But they had no way of proving at that moment that she was not the true winner and had to present her the women's award for first place. In later reviews of movies and photos taken throughout the race, she was never seen, and the rightful woman winner was eventually recognized as the true winner. However, the imposter had deprived the winner of her deserved moment of glory. Thankfully, that was re-enacted a few days later, but I'm sure it was not the same as it would have been on her day of accomplishment.

The imposter's name was Rosie Ruiz. It was later found that she had similarly cheated in the marathon in which she had supposedly qualified to participate in the Boston Marathon. Another woman that had done the same thing confessed that the two of them had cheated together at the New York Marathon a few months earlier.

A cute thing happened at the Boston Marathon the following year. A true marathon runner commenced the run, quickly exited from the race, and hurriedly took a cab to a point near the finish line. Quickly running through the finish line, he proclaimed that he should receive the Rosie Ruiz Award for the new record time!

A month or so later, I received a nice certificate for having been a participant in the event. It showed the elapsed time in which I had completed the race and my position in order of completion. Like all of the other marathons, it took several days to recover but it had been worth it. And I wish I could do it all again!

# 47. BREAKING THREE HOURS

IN THE YEAR 490 BC, The Persian army marched upon the Greek city of Athens. The Athenians, although heavily outnumbered, surprisingly won the ensuing land battle after the Persians split their forces, sending their naval armada to take the city from the sea. The epic battle occurred near the town of Marathon.

A runner named Pheidippides was then allegedly dispatched to quickly carry the news of the victory back to Athens, a distance of about twenty-five miles. Upon this favorable notification, the city forces then refused to surrender to the Persian naval force, and the Persians failed in their attempt to defeat the Greek nation. As a result of the extreme exertion required, the runner Pheidippides is said to have immediately died following delivery of this crucial message.

This famous and popular story is most likely fictitious in its details although Pheidippides was a historical figure that served as a runner in this battle. In 1896, the story inspired the inclusion of a foot race of a distance of approximately twenty-five miles as one of the athletic events during the return of the Olympic games in modern times. In honor of the pivotal battle that led to the Greek victory, the running event was named the Marathon. The event was subsequently changed to a distance to 26 miles and 385 yards (26.22 miles).

Other than occasionally seeing some reference to the Boston Marathon or perhaps of the event occurring in the Olympics, I had never known anything about marathons. However, in 1978, a fellow instructor pilot at NAS Meridian, Captain Jim Collins, suggested that a few of us begin training for the annual Marine Corps Marathon at Washington, DC that coming November. Having recently undergone a divorce and needing some distracting activity, I accepted the challenge and commenced the training.

My basic instructions regarding training were to alternate long and short runs during the week and to include one long run, and have it continue increasing in length as the weeks passed. Another point must be emphasized for anyone commencing any exercise regimen or activity. Begin with small and manageable efforts and increase the activity gradually. For someone that has not been running previously, simply jogging for a quarter of a mile or so might be a very adequate way to begin. If that goes comfortably well, increase it to half of a mile the next day and so on. The point is to give the body time to adjust to the new loads being placed upon it. I can still remember the first time I ran four miles, I was so proud that I told a friend, "I think I could have kept going."

And don't fall for that "no pain, no gain" crap. Sore muscles the next day are an indication that you overdid something in your training, whatever activity you are pursuing. If you encounter any significant soreness, back off from the training and let the body catch up before pushing on again. Be patient. It takes months to develop the strength and endurance to run long distances comfortably.

Once I was in good condition, and for subsequent marathons, I settled into a standard training regimen. It consisted of running distances of four and eight miles on alternate days, commencing on Tuesday of each week. My long run would then occur on Sunday afternoon, followed by a day off from training on Monday before commencing training again the next day.

It is not required that one run the full twenty-six miles during training. I tried to begin training early enough that I would be able to run three twenty-mile runs as my weekly long runs prior to the race. The week before the event, I would run only sixteen miles for my long run. Then, in the final week, I ran distances such as four, three, two miles, and finally no run at all on the day before the race. Meanwhile, I would have been eating good, carbohydrate-laden meals. On the morning of the marathon, I was always so pumped-up and full of energy and fitness that I felt like I could jump over the moon. Fifteen to twenty miles later was a different matter!

Although I completed that first marathon, I was plagued by a muscle cramp for the last eight miles, resulting in a poor elapsed time for the event. However, I improved with each subsequent marathon and qualified to run the prestigious Boston Marathon in April of 1980, slightly less than two years after commencing long distance running. I eventually ran about twenty marathons and was fortunate to be able to finish them all.

Having come close to completing the distance within a time of three hours a few times during 1980, I was determined to run it within three hours or less during the coming year of 1981. I ran the Mardi Gras Marathon for the second time in February of that year. I was in really great condition and probably would have run it in less than three hours, had it not been for a twenty miles per hour headwind (!) the entire way. The Mardi Gras Marathon at the time was conducted across Lake Ponchartrain, commencing two miles north of the lake and completing two miles south of the lake.

My next marathon would be the Mississippi Marathon during the coming December of 1981. In fact, it would occur on my forty-fourth birthday. Tom Griffin, a fellow runner in Meridian, wanted to run a marathon, never having done so. He asked my advice regarding training and further asked to run the event alongside me as he knew I was acquainted with pacing and general strategy. Tom was a few years older than me and of the same height, but weighed perhaps ten pounds less than I did. He was an excellent runner and could beat me in all of the shorter distances.

On the appointed date, we arrived in Jackson for the event. Both of us were very well-trained and reasonably confident in achieving our goals, his of a successful completion of the marathon, and mine of running it in less than three hours.

Running the distance in a time of three hours requires a pace of approximately 6.9 minutes per mile. If you, the reader, are in fairly good condition, you can probably run a mile in that amount of time. However, as you try to continue running subsequent miles at the same pace, you will find within a few miles that it is quite difficult in your un-trained state. And you can forget about trying to run ten miles in seventy minutes.

My strategy contained two components. The first was the use of what is called drafting, during which one runner follows closely and directly behind the lead runner. Even when running at only about ten miles per hour, wind resistance becomes significant over a long distance. Alternating the lead position every five miles enabled each of us to conserve just a little bit of energy that would have otherwise been expended in overcoming this wind resistance.

The second component of strategy concerned the pace. I planned to run the race at an average pace of 6.8 minutes per mile. This would enable me to arrive at the final two miles with an extra two minutes available to cover these miles. It turned out that I would certainly need them.

I must emphasize that the running pace and goal of a three-hour marathon are pitiful goals compared to Olympic-quality athletes. Those runners run the entire race at five minutes per mile and complete the distance in two hours and ten minutes or so! Comparing me to those athletes would be like comparing me to Michael Jordan in one-on-one in basketball. So don't think I was under any delusion that I was a great runner. On the other hand, for the normal, everyday sort of person that I was, a three-hour marathon would be a very noteworthy achievement, particularly for someone in his mid-forties. If you don't think so, take up the sport and tell me three years from now how close you are to running a three-hour marathon.

There are several cute sayings that marathon runners occasionally use. One is, "If you miss two days of training in a row, you're out of shape." The point is that the runner must pay the dues in training. Another is, "If you are tired after the first ten miles, you're in trouble." I would not normally begin getting tired until about fifteen miles into the race.

Another somewhat well-known point about running marathons is what is termed "hitting the wall." It turns out that even when well-trained, the human body usually runs out of readily-available energy after about eighteen to twenty miles. The runner must then commence digging deeper somewhere within the body itself to come up with the energy to continue the run. I don't pretend to understand the physiology of it. All I know is that it becomes extremely difficult, to the point of aching all over, to continue running for the last six to eight miles.

Before Tom and I commenced our run in Jackson, Mississippi that day, I told him, "Tom, we will run together as long as we can, but eventually one of us will probably be unable to maintain the pace. When that occurs, the other runner will have to proceed on his own." And off we went.

Sure enough, at around eighteen miles, I found that I could no longer hold the target pace and had to drop behind. I was beginning to hit the wall and within a few miles I was struggling just to keep running. Being the great Marine that I was, however, I continued doing my best.

A point about running marathons is that a runner can always run faster at any given moment. However, by doing so, the time for the overall run will be increased. The run must be performed at a pace that will provide the least overall amount of time to complete the race. If one runs too slowly, he or she will enjoy a much easier marathon run but will not accomplish the best possible time. Likewise, attempting to run too fast will cause one to run out of gas before the finish the line and will also require more time.

The successful runner must know his body well enough to choose a pace that will accomplish the distance in the minimum amount of time. Ideally, this would result in the runner passing out as he or she comes across the finish line, having used up all of the energy he or she had available. Okay, so I'm exaggerating a little...but the point is valid.

Finally, with less than a mile to go, I looked down at my watch while running alone through the streets of Jackson. It was going to be close so I exerted just a little more effort. Within a few moments, I began graying out as my vision began to falter. I had to slow down just a little to let my vision return to normal and keep from passing out. Looking down at my watch a few moments later, I again tried to run a little faster. Once again, I began graying out and had to slow down. It was only a few hundred more feet to the turn off from this street, followed by a few hundred feet more to the finish line.

As I made the turn, it was literally all downhill now. I passed under the clock and banner in what I saw was less than three hours. A few moments later I found the official time to have been two hours, fifty-nine minutes and two seconds (2:59:02). I had done it! For the record, Tom Griffin had completed a few minutes ahead of me during his first marathon. Hey, the guy was good! You have to give him credit.

One of my good friends, Bobby Boyd, had dropped out of the race earlier due to an injury and saw me come across the line. He knew I was trying to break three hours that day. Later, he half-jokingly said, "Larry, I saw you come across the finish line. And it's not worth it." He was referring to the degree of fatigue that I showed at that moment.

I disagree. That was my goal. I had trained for it and had made the best possible effort I could have made. And I was fortunate to be able to accomplish it. It was the only sub-three-hour marathon I ever ran. And it's history and I'm proud of it. Setting goals and paying the price for their accomplishment is what character is all about.

I give thanks to God for giving me enough drive to set worthwhile goals, enough physical strength and endurance to achieve them, and enough character within to make the sacrifices required to make them happen.

I just wish I could have been as successful in all of the goals of my life.

# 48. THE PRAYING DENTIST

I REMEMBER THE FIRST TIME I saw Captain "Dutch" Short. It was in 1983, the day of the National Prayer Breakfast during my last tour of duty at Naval Air Station Meridian. I didn't know who he was at the time. There may have been a couple of dozen military personnel gathered there that morning, and by chance I found myself seated next to him. I probably never even noticed that he was a navy captain.

The first time that I noticed him was during a prayer. Someone else was leading the prayer, but I could hear him praying under his breath, not intending to be heard by others. Normally in such situations, I believe that nearly everyone, if not everyone, sits quietly, listening to the prayer being offered at the time.

It caused my eyebrows to rise slightly, as I felt that I was in the presence of a veritable saint among men. I could feel the deep religious aura that the man lent to the gathering, without trying to do so at all. I may not have even spoken to him that day, and there was no reason to suspect that our lives would ever cross again.

In December of that year, I visited the station infirmary for my annual flight physical. Sitting in the dentist chair for my examination, I was mildly surprised when my prayer companion friend walked into the room. Dr. Short, or Captain Short, as you please, was pleasant with me as he conducted his examination and I was soon on my way to other phases of the exam. I don't recall more about the examination and I don't remember if I required any attention at all.

Six months later, I retired from the Marine Corps on 1 July 1983. I had not thought of the captain since the day of the flight physical and I would not think of him again for another four years. Sometime around the summer of 1987, however, I felt that I needed a dental checkup, not having had one since retiring four years earlier. By that time, Captain Short had also retired. I had recognized his name on his dental office building in a nearby shopping center, near the post office that I occasionally used. So I called his office and scheduled an appointment.

I was in for a surprise! No one anywhere likes to go to a dentist. In fact, it can be stated even more strongly. Everyone hates to go to a dentist. We can all identify with that feeling. After all, our mouths are one of the most tender and sensitive places on our entire bodies. And who wants someone poking around inside them with sharp objects, or administering shots or doing a variety of other very unpleasant things to them after we've protected them so well all of our lives!

But as Dr. Short welcomed me into his office, this all went out the window. His open and friendly manner cast all of my anxieties aside, and I relaxed in his presence as though I had been a friend of his for years. After a few moments, I sat in his chair as we continued our conversation. I reminded him that he had seen me as a patient when we were both still on active duty. Within a few minutes, he introduced me to his assistant, a lovely, quiet-spoken, and pleasant lady named Faye Massey, who would contribute greatly in the coming weeks by helping to put me at ease as a new patient under their care.

After telling Dr. Short that I remembered him from the naval air station, we made small talk for several minutes as we rehashed some of the pleasant memories that our years of service had provided. Finally, he said something to the effect of, "Let's have a look inside," and he commenced a general inspection of my teeth.

When he finished, he said, "Larry, you need quite a bit of work. When you were on active duty, there were limits to the care we were allowed to provide, but the work should really be done now." He then described the various problems that I had and what he felt should be done to correct them. I replied, "Dr. Short, you decide what needs to be done and do the job as if you were working on your own brother." He said that he would do so, and furthermore, that he would do "Cadillac work at Ford prices." I told him I would like for him to begin at his earliest convenience, and that I would be available when he was ready. The final point that he made to me was, "When I get through with you, you will carry your teeth with you to the grave."

He did no more work on that first visit, and I left the office feeling very pleased to have chosen Dr. Short as my dentist. I felt very comfortable with my decision, knowing that I would be in the best of hands for the duration of his care. So for the next month or so, I would see him maybe once every week while he made various improvements to my dental condition. Dr. Short liked to work in the evenings, and this went well with my work schedule as a teacher, my new profession following military retirement.

I mentioned a surprise earlier, meaning how comfortable the experience of the visit had been. But once Dr. Short was ready to commence actual work on his patients, he would always begin with a word of prayer. And there, as you were laid back in his chair, with him seated by your right side and Faye on the other, he would lay the palm of his hand softly on your shoulder and offer the most sincere and beautiful prayer that one could imagine.

He prayed that his hands might provide the care that I might need, and that his hands would be guided to provide the absolute best services that a dentist could offer. I don't mean to put words into his mouth and I could never recount the beauty of his words. I'm just trying to provide an idea of the sincerity of the prayers he always made before beginning work on his patients.

Then, as Doctor Short would commence, he might say, "This might sting just a little," as he gave some numbing shot. I merely lay there with my mouth open fully wide, relaxing, knowing that I was in the best care imaginable. There may have been moments of minor discomfort, but it was no problem as I realized the importance of what he was doing for me. And Faye was right there to perform on cue, providing comforting assistance whenever needed. Their performance as a team went beyond the mere technical aspects of their work. They were true artists when the total effect of their efforts was considered.

This continued at one evening per week for several weeks, with each visit exactly like the last, until he had finally completed the service regimen he had outlined for me. I gladly paid the bill and walked away in far better dental health than I had probably ever known. But the real joy was in having become a patient and friend of this fine and wonderful man.

In our conversations before his work each time, he would ask about my life and work and other activities. I was running marathons at the time and he was becoming a runner as well. He invited me to his home on a few Saturdays and we would run a few miles together. Years later, when introducing me to some new assistant, he would exaggerate the contributions I had made to his running abilities. By that time, he had run the Blue Angel Marathon at Pensacola and perhaps another one or two. He looked up to my running accomplishments, however, knowing that I was a more experienced runner, having been running for several more years than him.

Over the years, I continued visiting his office for regular checkups, having my teeth cleaned, etc. And, do you know what? I believe that I was his very best friend. Well, certainly I wasn't, but that is how he always made me feel. And I'm sure that he made hundreds of other patients feel the same way.

By last fall (2011), it had been twenty-four years since I had made my initial visit to his office. I was growing older, but more worrisome to me was that my dentist was also growing older. We had noted that we were nearly the same age, with him being almost exactly one year older than me.

I was afraid he would retire before I stopped needing him so I would tell him of how important his work was to me and that I hoped that he could continue his practice. I'm sure my words had no influence on his actions. He worked because he enjoyed serving others. It was more than a job to him. Just as Jesus had been a healer, so was Dr. Short. And in his work life as in his daily life, he was serving his Lord each day as a disciple, spreading his love and witness to those that came under his care.

This past Sunday, as I read the paper, I happened to glance at the obituary page. Suddenly I saw his picture and name and I felt a deep blow to my body. I called my wife and we mourned the loss of our wonderful friend and dentist. We had shared his services with other members of our family, including some of our adult children and my wife's aged mother. He was loved and appreciated by all that he served.

He was a very special man to me, although our paths crossed only a few times outside of his office. But he was a person I had come to love, and was one of my dwindling ties to the years when I was serving my country.

George Allen "Dutch" Short, Captain, United States Navy, Retired, will be much missed by all that knew him. If dentists are useful in heaven, he will certainly be laying his hands on shoulders there as well, as he begins his heavenly duties.

As life goes on for those of us left behind, we whose lives he touched are better for the life that he lived. My final wish in these regards is that my life will have made a similar contribution, however diminished, compared to this great man.

# 49. "FINAL FINAL"

THERE WERE PROBABLY FIVE OR six small outlying airfields in the Pensacola area to accommodate the large number of students undergoing primary flight training. The reason is that if there are too many planes practicing landings at a given field, too much time is spent just flying back and forth, up and down the field, with little time practicing the critical portion of the landing.

The most important part of landing a plane is the descending half-circle turn, culminating in the straight-in, final descent to touching down on the runway. The commencement point of this turn is called the 180 for the number of degrees of turn remaining to land the plane. It is followed by the 90 and then the 45 as the descending turn continues.

If there is no appreciable wind, landing the plane involves just the runway, the descending turn, and the plane itself. Wind conditions can add a significant degree of difficulty, however. The critical issue regarding wind is how much of it is blowing across the runway and in which direction.

If the wind is blowing in the direction of the turn, it is called an overshooting crosswind, the worst kind. This crosswind tends to blow the plane past the extended runway line and requires a higher angle of bank to complete the turn before landing. Flying at a higher angle of bank increases the possibility of stalling the plane. Stalling the plane at such a low altitude would most likely be followed by a crash. Many a student has received a down on a check flight for inability to land successfully in an overshooting crosswind condition.

The attrition rate for Navy and Marine Corps student pilots during my training was probably around thirty percent, if not slightly higher. The most common cause for attrition was that the student was not aerodynamically adaptable, which simply means that his flying abilities were not up to the required standards.

When a student receives a down on a check flight he (or she, nowadays) is usually given two extra instructional flights, and then undergoes a second check flight. If this becomes a pattern for a student, he is generally dropped from the training program. It is better to weed him (or her) out at this point than to have them crash a plane at some later time, possibly killing themselves and others.

Occasionally a student decides to terminate the training at his or her own request. This is called dropping on request, or DOR, for short. I remember when one of my best friends, Ensign Warren Howell, DOR'd during basic jet training. I asked him why and he said, "It isn't any fun trying to fly while the instructor is continually criticizing your mistakes." I tried to explain that this was his job and that we all experienced it to some degree. But he was intent on quitting the program.

There is the popular "John Wayne" image of the jet pilot flying his high performance jet plane heroically through the skies. And flying eventually does become that. But first you have to go through a long and reasonably difficult program until you know enough and are good enough to be that John Wayne. Maybe Warren was a weak student that wasn't doing well. Perhaps he had an overly-demanding and critical instructor. I don't know. But within a few days he was gone from our lives.

When performing practice landings at a field having a control tower, a request to land was made at the 180-degree position, including the statement that the landing gear was down and that a touch and go landing was requested. After completion of all desired touch and go landing practice, the last landing request was altered to include the words, "final landing," indicating that this would be the last landing and the flight would be over.

After completing the four to five month portion of their training at NAS Meridian, the students would be transferred back to Pensacola for gunnery and carrier qualification training in Training Squadron Four (VT-4). It became a tradition for the student, on his last landing approach at NAS Meridian, to modify the landing request to include the words, "final final."

Approximately eight years of my military career were spent as a basic jet flight instructor at Meridian. During that period I accumulated over 3,600 hours of flight time in the T-2 Buckeye jet trainer. I estimate that I observed at least 10,000 student landings from the back seat during some 2,600 instructional flights. As an instructor, I observed the landing approaches over the student's left shoulder during the turn. My left hand was always just inches behind the power lever and my right hand inches behind the control stick, ready to take over at any moment while saying, "I've got it."

During my last months of active duty, though, I was flying a twin-engine "prop" plane, the C-1A, on miscellaneous missions back and forth to various naval bases. Its wings could be folded overhead and it was designed for use as a cargo plane operating from aircraft carriers. Flying this plane provided its own air of romance and I enjoyed the missions as they were similar to flying the R4D Hummer in Vietnam back in 1970. But there finally came the time for my last military flight.

A Navy pilot friend, Rich Powell, once told me that the two worst days in a pilot's life are the day when he steps into a plane knowing it will be his last flight, and the day when he steps into a plane not knowing it will be his last flight.

I had the good fortune to know when my last flight was occurring. I had returned to NAS Meridian from a flight to NAS Pensacola and entered the break over the runway when only a few jets were in the landing pattern. Flying downwind, I completed the landing checklist and made my call to the tower, "McCain Tower, this is Navy 123, abeam with gear down, for a 'final final.'"

I was cleared to land and moments later that portion of my life was over, forever. There would be no more flights on dark, moonless nights, no more descending through the clouds and fog, hoping to see the field after breaking out underneath, no more hurling myself at the enemy with guns blazing or looking through a bombsight. Yes, all of those things were over. But I would love to have been a second lieutenant on that day, commencing it all over again.

But I had served my country and was proud to have done so. And today, even at the age of 74, if you ever really, really need an attack pilot, or even just a jet flight instructor, I will be glad to put the flight gear back on and help you all I can.

# 50. "WHAT MIGHT HAVE BEEN"

This story is about something that happened just a few days before leaving Lexington for the Marine Corps in September of 1962. The reason that it is placed at the end is that these memories lay dormant for nearly forty years, and they contained a critical moment that could have resulted in immense changes in the course of my life.

At the age of ten, my father moved our family away from Cumberland, Kentucky, a Harlan County town in the hills of southeastern Kentucky. He had been working at nearby Lynch, a "coal mining camp" as such towns were called. The family moved to another coal mining camp about seventy miles away by the name of Wheelwright, still in eastern Kentucky. After graduating from high school there, I attended Caney Junior College (now Alice Lloyd College), a small liberal arts school some thirty miles away. After graduating from "Caney," I attended the University of Kentucky until earning my BS and MS degrees in Mechanical Engineering in 1961 and 1962.

I've always been embarrassed to have gone to school for so long but there were reasons. When I commenced junior college, I knew absolutely no math or science, whatsoever. I had always read a lot and had learned other things but I knew almost nothing in those two areas. Accordingly, I made poor grades in those courses in junior college, and had to repeat several of them at the university since I had chosen to major in engineering.

It was really like commencing college all over again. To add to the problem, I didn't take a full academic load each semester due to working at a U.S. Public Health Service Hospital for four years for room and board while in Lexington. However, the bottom line was that I eventually received two degrees in engineering and as we all know, education is something that can never be taken from us. It served me well during my military career and has enabled me to teach math and physics in community colleges since military retirement in 1983. If I had those decisions to make over, I would make the same ones again. Like my son said a few years ago, "You made some good decisions when you were young, Dad."

During those college years, I dated several girls and even fell in love once. Unfortunately, the feelings were not reciprocated and it took me a few years to eventually get over it. Finally, as the fall of 1962 approached, I remember thinking to myself, "Well, I've gone through my college years without finding the girl I will marry." I accepted that and thought something would just have to happen further down the road of life. I worked on my thesis project all summer and finally commenced writing it as September approached. I had military orders to report to Quantico, Virginia on September 16th and there was no grace period involved. I had to be there on that date.

I was dating a very pretty girl that summer but deep feelings were not involved. She left for home at the end of the summer term and I never saw her again. And then one day, only one week before leaving Lexington, I saw Pat Fraley on campus, a girl from my home town. We had graduated from the same high school, with Pat graduating two years after me. Her college years had been interrupted when her father had been injured in a coal mining accident. So here she was, five years out of high school and still in college. After talking for a few minutes, we made a date for a movie the coming Saturday night. It was to be the last weekend of my college years.

I had only seen her twice since graduation from high school. The first time had been nearly three years before, when I was home from school for Christmas. I saw her at the church we had always attended and ended up driving her home. It had happened too suddenly, however, and I failed to take the initiative to inquire about seeing her at school.

We didn't attend the same school; she attended Georgetown College about twelve miles north of Lexington. I had to get back to Lexington for my job the next day and didn't take advantage of the opportunity to inquire about possibly seeing her at college. Like I say, I blew it. Of course, she may have already had a boy friend at the time. I will never know.

I saw her again the next summer when I stopped by her home one afternoon and talked with her for a few minutes on her front porch. But this time I made no move because the girl I had fallen in love with had just broken off our relationship. I was in no mood to think of another girl at all.

So look what fate had dealt me. Here I was having a date with someone special, but on an evening just four days before leaving Lexington and my college years! And why do I refer to this girl as special? I had read a book a few years earlier about courtship and marriage. I've always remembered that there were five considerations regarding the possibility of a serious relationship. They were: age, education, religion, geographical, and social backgrounds. Those considerations didn't occur to me on the night I was with her. It never entered my mind of how well we fulfilled those criteria for one another until looking back on it nearly fifty years later.

Because, after all, we had grown up literally only two or three miles apart, and there were less than two years difference in our ages. We had attended the same church and high school, and we had both been children of coal miners from the hills of eastern Kentucky. That was as "five for five" as five could be. There was good chemistry between us the evening we were together, but the thoughts mentioned above did not occur to me during the only date we would ever have.

A contributing point is that I had already given up on the "boy meets girl during college" thing. I remember the fleeting thought going into this date that, even though I had admired her years before, I shouldn't think anything important was going to happen. I viewed it as a one-time date with an old acquaintance and then I would be off to the Marine Corps.

A few years ago I mentioned this girl and our date to my son. He was not impressed. He said that nothing may have come of it anyway. And even if it had, there could still have been a divorce like he and I had both been through by then. He had lost his faith in the possible goodness of "what might have been."

When I look back at the time of my date with Pat, I know there were several reasons that contributed to my failure to follow up on the date. After all, I was turning in a thesis two days later and I would have my oral exam just two days after that. I was quitting my job at the hospital, selling my motorcycle, and making a major change in my life. When I told this to my son, he said, "You had a lot on your plate, Dad." That was true.

The Saturday evening finally arrived. I showered, dressed, and drove into Lexington and picked her up at her dormitory. She was beautiful in a black dress that showed her off very well. I don't remember the drive into town, anything about the movie or the drive away from the movie. We drove out to Jerry's Drive-In on the beltway on the north side of Lexington and sat talking while enjoying a coke for a few minutes. Then we drove back across town, parked in a nice place on campus near her dorm, and sat continuing our conversation.

After several minutes, I scooted over closer to her and we ended up enjoying a few very nice kisses. And this is where I encountered my critical moment, a subject of which I wrote in an earlier story. It was the moment when I should have said, after our first kiss, something like, "Mmm, Pat, that was really good. Pat, I've told you that I'm leaving within a few days to join the Marine Corps, hopefully to become a pilot. I would love to get to write to you occasionally in the hopes of seeing you again someday. What do you think about it?" That would have put the ball into her court and given her the chance to give an answer.

The worst case is that she could have said something like, "Well, Larry, I'm going to have a lot of tough courses, and I don't think I should get involved with someone right now." That would have been a nice way of just saying, "No." Or she could have said, "That would be nice." Or, best of all, she could have said, "I would like that very much."

I think the answer would have fallen somewhere between the last two responses. The problem is, however, she never had the opportunity to give any of these answers. I failed in my critical moment by saying nothing of substance, and shortly after that I took her back to her dorm. And as far as I know, I never thought of her again for nearly forty years.

That thought occurred around the year 2000 when I was at the annual Wheelwright Day celebration in Lexington. I saw one of my good friends from high school who had dated her at that time. I knew he had never married her and I asked if he knew anything of what had happened in her life over the years. He said he had heard that she had died.

After that, I would think of her occasionally, remembering what a deserving young woman she had been, and that she should have had gotten a better break in life. And several years later, after thinking of her again, it finally dawned on me what a great opportunity I had had on that September night in 1962.

It was very likely that she didn't have a special boy friend at the time. And there I was, freshly educated with an MS in engineering, a hometown boy that she could have related to. I believe she would have been inclined to give our letter-writing relationship a chance. And if it had happened, there is a fairly good possibility that we would have married.

The end of my initial obligated tour of military duty coincided with my return from my first year in Vietnam in the early summer of 1967. I had planned to leave the Marine Corps at that time and return to the hills of Kentucky. I had been offered a position to teach math and physics at Caney Junior College where I had graduated ten years earlier.

I had always known I wanted to be a teacher someday but it was not to be, at least not at that time. When my Mississippi-reared wife took one look at those hills, she said she could never live there. So I opted to stay in the Marine Corps, and that is when my first tour as a flight instructor commenced. If I had married Pat instead, the move back to Kentucky would have occurred, and that is likely where I would have been living for the past forty-five years.

Looking back on memories such as this, one is tempted to say they wish this or that would have happened. But it didn't and there was a marriage to another pretty young woman, and children were born and reared. And there are so many things I've done in my life that would not have happened if had married Pat instead.

I finally realized that all I could say about this event and others like it is, "I wish I had always made the best decisions during my life, knowing what I knew at the time, whatever the situation may have been."

That would have covered all of the bases without any guilt trips for the thoughts of, "what might have been."

END

*Commanding General*
*Fleet Marine Force Atlantic*
*takes pleasure in presenting*

FIRST LIEUTENANT LARRY R. GIBSON 086255 USMCR

*the Navy "E"*
*for your excellent demonstration*
*of a high degree of proficiency in*
*weapons delivery in the conduct*
*of competitive exercises in*

SPECIAL WEAPONS

*This commendable exhibition of*
*professional competence and skill*
*meets the high standards which*
*are traditional in Naval Aviation*

A. L. BOWSER
LT. GENERAL
U.S. MARINE CORPS

DEBRIEFER _____ TIME _____ DATE 26 Sept 69
SQUADRON VMA-223 CALL SIGN Hellborne 151 MSN NO 6151 FLT 152/1
T/O 0633 LAND 0748 TOTAL TIME 2.B

PILOTS        AIRCRAFT
Maj Palmer    WL 10      DASC Dng the     TIME 0645
Gibson        WL 17      CONTROLLER Sawtooth 48-1 TIME 0650-0720
                        TYPE CONTROLLER OV-10 FACA
                        TYPE MISSION DAS

TOT              DESCRIPTION        COORDINATES      PROVINCE
0650-0720    enemy position     YD 023 626       I Corps
                    55

TGT TERRAIN Rolling hills TGT WX Clear     VISIBILITY 15+
REL ANGLE 30°  PASSES 4  INTERVAL 30 sec  REL ALT 3000 AGL
                                          MIN ALT 1500 AGL
ENROUTE ALT 18.5   RETURN ALT 15.5   TGT AIRSPEED 450 KTS
ORDNANCE 12 D2W/Y   EXPENDED 11 D2W/Y   JETTISONED None
ORDNANCE RTB 1 D2W/Y   DUDS (SEE NOTE # 1) None
BDA 100/100%       ADDITIONAL 1 bunker uncovered

SECONDARY EXPLOSIONS None   NUMBER OF _____   SIZE OF _____
UNIT SUPPORTED 3rd Mar Div   OPERATION IDAHO (LEAVE BLANK)
ENROUTE WEATHER _____
REMARKS: _____
(REFERENCE NOTE #3)

NOTE #1: DUD REPORT LOCATION _____ REASON FOR DUD _____
         RECOVERED? FUZE (DELAY/ARM DELAY)
NOTE #2: SCR HERE TARGET _____ TIME _____ BDA DIVERTED _____
NOTE #3: ORDNANCE EFFECTIVENESS _____
NOTE #4: CONTROLLER EFFECTIVENESS _____

(A) HOSTILE FIRE        YES  NO    FILE FORM WITH BARREL
(B) AIRBORST            YES  NO    FILE FORM WITH BARREL
(C) ACFT HIT            YES  NO    FILE FLASH REPORT WITH BARREL
(D) RECON INSERT/EXTRACT YES NO    CIRCLE ONE/COORD
(E) BDA REPORTED        YES  NO    IF ADDITIONAL CIRCLE
(F) ABORT               YES  NO    ACFT MALFUNCTION/NO DROP
(G) DIVERT              YES  NO    GIVE REASON BELOW

# C-RATIONS

C-rations were utilized by military personnel serving in Vietnam (and elsewhere) when regularly-prepared meals could not be provided. These meals were provided as individual rations, containing approximately 1200 calories per meal. Each meal was individually packed and contained an "M" unit, a "B" unit and a "D" unit. The various units are described as follows.

The following material was copied from "Wikipedia", the free internet encyclopedia.

# C-RATION MENUS

The "M" unit came in 12 basic varieties in three menus of four different entrees, supplemented by "Alternate" variant entrees:

**M-1**: Beefsteak, Chicken or Turkey loaf, Chopped Ham & Eggs, or Ham Slices    (Cooked in Juices or Fried). **M-1A**: Tuna fish.

**M-2**: Meat Chunks with Beans in Tomato Sauce, Ham & Lima Beans, Beef Slices with Potatoes in Gravy, or Beans with Frankfurter Chunks in Tomato Sauce. **M-2A**: Spaghetti with Meatballs in Tomato Sauce.
**M-3**: Beef in Spiced Sauce, Boned Chicken or Turkey, Chicken with Noodles in Broth, or Pork Steak Cooked in Juices. **M-3A:** Meat Loaf.

The "B" unit came in three different varieties:

**B-1**: Seven Crackers and two Chocolate Discs (Types: Solid Chocolate, Chocolate Crème, or Chocolate Coconut). Peanut Butter Spread.

**B-2**: Four Hardtack Biscuits (often referred to by the troops as "John Wayne  cookies") and a cookie sandwich or fudge disc.
     Cheese Spread (Types: Processed Cheese with Pimentos, or Processed Cheese with Caraway Seeds). **Spread Alternate**: Plain Cheddar Cheese.

**B-3**: Four cookies and a packet of Cocoa powder.
     Jam Spread (Types: Apple, Mixed Berry, Seedless Blackberry, Mixed Fruit,    Grapes or Strawberry).

The "D" unit came in three different types:

**D-1 (Fruit):** Halved Apricots, Sliced Peaches, Quartered Pears, Fruit Cocktail. **D-1A: (Fruit):** Applesauce,.

**D-2 (Cake):** Pound Cake, Fruitcake, Cinnamon Nut Roll. **D-2A (Cake):** Date Pudding and Orange Nut Roll.

**D-3 (Bread):** White Bread. (There were no alternates).

Each menu was grouped by their unit number (i.e., M-1, B-1 and D-1 items were grouped together). As an example, the jam in the B-3 unit was meant to be spread on the White Bread in the D-3 unit. Alternate items (designated with an "A" suffix) were used to provide variety and reduce the monotony. For variety, the M-1 and M-3 units (since they both used small cans) were often switched.

The "B-unit's" **Crackers & Candy** can was lined with a piece of corrugated cardboard to protect the contents from damage. In the "D" –unit, the white bread came in one solid cylindrical piece wrapped in wax paper, while the pound cake, fruitcake, Orange Nut Roll, and Cinnamon Roll came wrapped in paper wrappers like cupcakes.,

The **Accessory Pack** came with salt, pepper, sugar, instant coffee, non-dairy creamer, two pieces of candy-coated chewing gum, a packet of toilet paper, a four-pack of commercial-grade cigarettes, and a book of 20 cardboard moisture-proof matches.

Typical commercial brands issued in the cigarette ration were: Camel, Chesterfield, Kent, Kool, Lucky Strike, Marlboro, Pall Mall, Salem, or Winston. Due to health concerns, cigarettes were eliminated from the accessory packs in 1975.